AMERICANS BEFORE COLUMBUS

ALSO BY ELIZABETH CHESLEY BAITY

AMERICA BEFORE MAN

SUN AND MOON   MAYAN GLYPH

AMERICANS
BEFORE COLUMBUS

BY ELIZABETH CHESLEY BAITY

ILLUSTRATED WITH DRAWINGS
AND MAPS BY C. B. FALLS AND
WITH 32 PAGES OF PHOTOGRAPHS

THE VIKING PRESS
NEW YORK

970.1   1.   Indians of North America
        2.   Indians of South America

CONTENTS

ILLUSTRATIONS
INDIAN ARTS AND ARCHITECTURE

PHOTOGRAPHS

DRAWINGS BY C. B. FALLS

Preface

During the decade since this book was first published, new discoveries have added enormously to the story of America's first men. Carbon-14 dating* has pin-pointed early finds with an accuracy impossible before 1950, when Dr. Willard Libby published his first list of C-14 dates. Recent C-14 dating takes our story back some forty-four thousand years, indicating that the Amerinds have been on the scene much longer than was once thought.

It is still believed that the early arrivals were migratory hunters, with some Mongoloid and some Caucasoid traits, who came across the Bering Strait region long ago. The Amerind is now given credit for inventing his early tools and weapons, though some cultural items are thought to have been brought in by later Asiatic arrivals. More and more Amerind experiments with basket-making, pottery, weaving, agriculture and architecture have been found. Archaeologists have learned much from an area called the Alaska-Chukchi province, where evidence from some five thousand years of indigenous culture shows that there were no hunting cultures on the Asiatic side which were directly ancestral to America's early herd-hunters.

The earlier theory of the Amerinds' late arrival in the New World was based partly on the fact that no Paleo-man skulls—beetle-browed, chinless, and prognathous—were found along the Bering route, but only those of modern or neo-man (*Homo sapiens sapiens*). Hundreds of skulls were measured, but since earlier researchers did not always follow the methods of modern

---

* Carbon-14 is a radioactive isotope of the element carbon, present in the air and thus absorbed into the bones of animals and fibers of plants. C-14 dating consists of Geiger-counting the scintillations of C-14 atoms in once-living material. Since the rate of decay of C-14 into nitrogen atoms is known, the time since the organic material tested was living can be measured, though not yet with exact reliability.

archaeologists, it was not realized that these modern-type skulls were embedded in geological strata laid down well before the supposed date of man's arrival at Bering Straits.

Recent C-14 dates show that neo-man was in the Americas while his kind were still disputing Europe and the Near East with Neanderthal man, here and there settling down to housekeeping instead of fighting. Perhaps the most fascinating of recent discoveries is that neo-man did not descend from beetle-browed Paleo-man but from ancestors smooth of brow and with determined chins which they were sticking into things as early as ninety-three thousand years ago, the provisional birth date now assigned to our species. Tool-making, we now know, is immensely older, pre-dating man himself.

Dr. and Mrs. L. S. B. Leakey, excavating since 1932 at Olduvai Gorge in Tanganyika, have uncovered the record of over a half million years of tool-making. The age of their finds was not always accepted by other experts, who usually arrived after sites were eroded. When in 1959 Mrs. Leakey discovered a new *Australopithecine* (Southern Ape) Clark Howell was on the spot in time to give this "missing link" his god-fatherly approval (January 1960, *Current Anthropology*). The Leakeys named their six-hundred-thousand-year-old youth of the Lower Pleistocene *Zinjanthropus*, or East Africa man. He had very large teeth, a small brain, and some manlike features found only in hominids of the Middle Pleistocene elsewhere, and he had his pebble tools all but in his hand. Some eighty feet of deposits containing pebble-tool cultures trace the development of these simple tools up to hand axes of types widely used in Eurasia's Old Stone Age.

Even East Africa Man, however, was a "Johnny-come-lately" in comparison with an individual who laid himself to rest during Europe's warm palmy days some ten million years ago, in what was to become a coal seam in middle Italy. In 1948 Dr. Johannes Hürzeler, of the 500-year-old University of Basel, Switzerland, thoughtfully re-examining a fossil jaw labeled *Oreopithecus* (Mountain Ape) found himself unable to classify it with the monkeys. During a ten-year search, both encouraged and frustrated by discoveries of some thirty specimens destroyed by mining operations, Dr. Hürzeler descended for his last afternoon in a coal mine about to be closed. Just as he was on the point of giving up, he flashed his light on the shaft roof and saw there, as if neatly sculptured, the fossilized remains of a complete Oreopithecus displaying a short, un-apelike face and hominid-type teeth and pelvic bones.

Though an extinct side branch rather than a direct ancestor of man, this hominid that is almost nine and a half million years older than any other known offers mute evidence that far from having descended from apes, man comes from an ancestral line which may have branched off from theirs by some fifty million or so years, according to Dr. Hürzeler—and, incidentally, to Charles Darwin himself. Labeled "the Abominable Coal-man" by wits, this early hominid calls for a re-examination of the time-scale allowed for man's evolution.

Acknowledgments for up-to-date materials and for expert assistance in assembling the newly added Chapter XIV will be found on page 266. The author also owes warm thanks to unnamed individuals for help during the past ten years, during which an avocational interest in American prehistory has developed, under the stimulus of work in Africa, Europe, and Asia, and study in the Anthropology Department of the University of North Carolina, into a more professional concern with cultural anthropology.

September 14, 1960
Geneva, Switzerland

ASIA

ARCTIC
OCEAN

MIGRATION FROM ASIA

ALASKA

ESKIMO

HUDSON
BAY

NORTH EAST

PACIFIC COAST

MOUND BUILDERS

PUEBLO

ATLANTIC
OCEAN

PACIFIC OCEAN

SOUTH EAST

GULF OF
MEXICO

AZTEC

CARIBBEAN SEA

MAYAN

ISTHMUS
OF PANAMA

NORTH
AMERICA

ISTHMUS OF PANAMA

CARIBBEAN SEA

ATLANTIC OCEAN

INCA

PACIFIC OCEAN

SOUTH AMERICA

SOME HIGH POINTS IN PREHISTORIC AMERICA (dates approximate)

	USUFRUCTIANS (people living off the land)		HERD HUNTERS		CULTURAL ADVANCES	CLIMATE CHANGES	CENTRAL and SOUTH AMERICA	SOME OLD WORLD EVENTS
	EAST	WEST	EAST	WEST				
1500	IROQUOIS / ALGONQUIAN TRIBES / MISSISSIPPIAN CULTURES	NORTHWEST COAST TRIBES / PUEBLOS	NO GAME HERDS IN EASTERN WOODLANDS	SIOUX and other PLAINS INDIANS	FEDERATIONS / Widespread trade, etc. / TEMPLE MOUNDS	Continuing slow warming up	AZTECS / INCA CITIES / MAYAS	Age of Discovery / MIDDLE AGES
500		Anasazi Hohokam Mongollon (Ariz.)			CEREMONIAL MOUNDS	Mesothermal (med. temp., as we have today)	TOLTECS / INCAS / MAYA villages / RECORDS	Barbarian Invasions / ROMAN EMPIRE
A.D.								
B.C.	HOPEWELL CULTURE (Ohio) / ADENA people (Ohio) / Poverty Point / Indian Knoll	BASKET-MAKERS	Virginia fluted-point hunters	BISON HUNTERS / Plainview Scotts Bluff bison	CULTIVATION: corn, beans, squash / POTTERY and other crafts / PRIMITIVE CORN	Cold waves / Warmer	ARCHITECTURE ARTS, CRAFTS / ASTRONOMY / PYRAMIDS / CORN / POTTERY	ROMAN REPUBLIC / GREECE / Minoans, etc. / CHINA, INDUS, EGYPT, MESOPOTAMIA high cultures
5000	ALABAMA SHELL-MIDDEN CULTURES / Lamoka Lake / OLD COPPER CULTURE / Graham Cave	Cochise Seed Gatherers	Alabama fluted-point hunters	hunters	DOG / USE OF COPPER / ATLATL / BASKETRY / SEED GRINDING	Ice returns / Warmer	Guanaco hunting (S.A.) / Incipient Cultivation	Village culture / WEAVING, etc. / CERAMICS / AGRICULTURE / PLANT TENDING
10,000								

EXTINCTION OF THE GREAT PLEISTOCENE GAME ANIMALS (mammoth, horse, camel)

	Modoc Cave	Danger Cave	Bull Brook	Gypsum Cave		Ice returns	BIG-GAME HUNTERS	Post-glacial forests
10,000		DESERT CULTURE		Gypsum Cave sloth hunters	Fiber sandals (woven)	Ice returns		Food collecting / Microliths
				Folsom big-bison hunters / MIDLAND MAN (Clovis) / Lehner-Naco mammoth hunters	Clovis fluted stone points	Warming / Ice returns / Seas begin rise from 330 ft. below present level / Warmer		Big-game hunting / Magdalenian Period
15,000				Sandia Cave (N. M.)	PEBBLE TOOLS / BONE TOOLS (engraved)	Ice as far south as Long Island		Solutrean Period (brief)
20,000					PEBBLE TOOLS / BONE TOOLS		NEANDERTHALOID HYBRIDS?	Gravettian Period / Middle Aurignacian Period (skin clothing, etc.) (Adaptation to cold)
30,000		TULE SPRINGS MAN			CHOPPERS / KNIVES of stone flakes		PUEBLA MAN (Valsequillo)	Last of Neanderthal Man / Cave Paintings (Cro-Magnon) / Ideas of after-life / OLD STONE AGE / Blade-tool industries / Chatelperronian / End of Acheuleo-Mousterian
40,000	LEWISVILLE MAN	SANTA ROSA MAN			PEBBLE TOOLS?			Homo sapiens s. / Homo sapiens & neanderthalensis / East Africa Man / Near-humans / Oreopithecus: earliest-known hominid (Italy) c. 10,000,000 B.C.

IVth Glacial 75,000 B.C.
IIIrd " 250,000 "
IInd " 750,000 "
Ist " 1,000,000 "

INDIAN ARTS AND ARCHITECTURE

The arts of the American Indians, like those of men in Europe, began as magic rites intended to aid hunting. Cro-Magnon men, the white-skinned people who lived in Europe twenty thousand years before Columbus, sought to snare the souls of animals by drawing pictures of the animals on the walls of caves and then performing magic rites before the pictures. These drawings are lifelike representations of bison and deer, faithfully drawn, yet showing such grace and strength that our best-trained artists today can hardly excel them. American Indians drew and carved art objects with the same intention and often with the same fidelity and grace, but there is something stranger to our eyes in the Indian arts than in those of Europe. The Indian arts have the feeling and characteristics of those that developed in Asia. Perhaps some of the earliest specimens were made in the Asiatic homeland, and it is possible that if some Chinese Columbus had discovered America, the beauty of Indian art would have been more fully appreciated and better preserved. But enough is left for us to trace the stages in the growth of Indian arts from magic rites to temples of almost unbelievable beauty.

When the white men came, Indian artists were working in all these stages. As we shall see, the Indians in what is now the United States had not advanced culturally as far as their cousins to the south. Their arts were more primitive, even more rudimentary than were the drawings of Cro-Magnon men. Indians farther south in Mexico had developed the great plastic arts—architecture, sculpture, and painting—to a high level of beauty. They had developed distinctive styles and had learned how to create within them objects and buildings of grace, profound spiritual meaning, and great magnificence. In the following section we will see briefly how these arts developed from their simple beginnings in craftsmanship and in magic rites.

STONE, SHELL, AND WOOD CARVING OF THE
MISSISSIPPI AND EASTERN FOREST REGIONS

STONE PIPE, HUMAN EFFIGY FROM THE ADENA MOUND, OHIO

The early people of the eastern woodlands and the Mississippi area made a great many pipes, some for religious and social rituals and some for burial with priests and rulers. Hundreds of them have been found that represent animals or birds (see the drawing on page 124), possibly the totem or "guardian" animals of the tribe.

The Mound Builder pipe showing the human figure is interesting because in design it is very like art objects made in southeastern Mexico. You may see this for yourself by comparing it with the clay figure on page 26.

Carved breast pendants such as that shown on page 124 were a part of the insignia of Mayan priests and rulers, as you can see from the mask-pendant on the Maize God on page 25. The Mound Builders carved breast ornaments of Gulf conch shells, many of them, like the one in the drawing, being pure Mexica-Mayan in design.

PAINTED STONE EFFIGY: LEBANON, TENNESSEE

Sandstone images of the same general style as the human figure pipes of
the Mound Builders have been found over a limited area centering in western
Tennessee. They are usually buried in pairs, male and female, in stone boxes.
The male effigy shown here, which was plowed up by a farmer in 1940,
represents anatomical detail much more realistically than is usual.

18

STONE, SHELL, AND WOOD CARVING OF THE
MISSISSIPPI AND EASTERN FOREST REGIONS

WAR CLUB, IROQUOIS, FOUND IN PENNSYLVANIA

The ball-headed club, used by the warriors of the Eastern Forests in hand-to-hand fighting, represents one of the practical uses to which wood-carving skill was put among the woodland tribes. This specimen, one of the finest yet found, has beauty of line and workmanship as well as perfect mechanical construction for its deadly purpose.

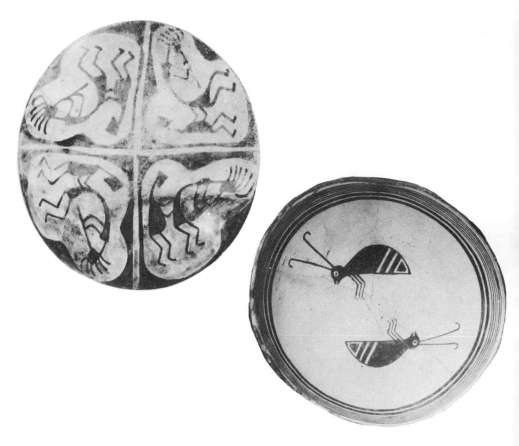

HOHOKAM BOWL: GILA PUEBLO, ARIZONA

Almost all of the hundreds of Indian tribes made and decorated pottery, and in many cases the making of ceramics became a real art form. Much funeralware was made to be burned or buried with the dead. Archaeologists have patiently fitted together jumbled pieces to give us examples of Indian ceramics over a two-thousand-year period. Painted and incised designs on pottery often imitated those on basketry and weaving, but this example from the ancient Hohokam people of Arizona, made around 800 A.D., shows human or near-human figures, one of whom may be wearing a mask or playing a musical instrument.

MIMBRES BOWL: MIMBRES VALLEY, NEW MEXICO

Indian vase painters usually followed conventional tribal designs which had magic ritualistic meanings and changed very slowly over centuries. A few gifted artists may have set their own mark on this art, however. The Mimbres bowls made in New Mexico in the twelfth century are quite distinctive, with their animal and insect figures entirely unlike geometrical basketry designs. Modern ceramic artists make bowls like this one.

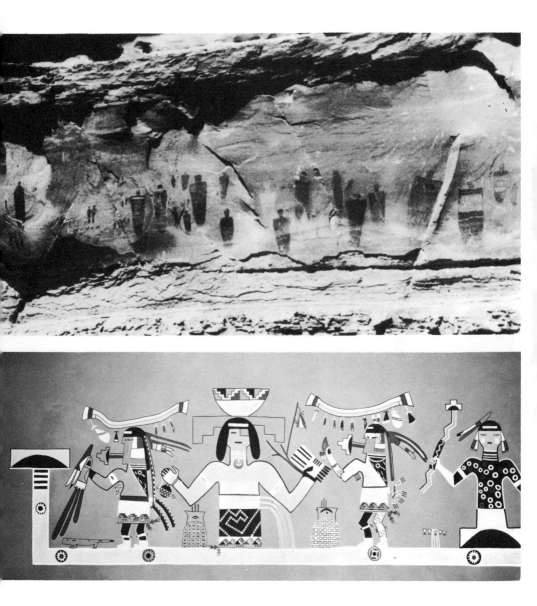

BASKETMAKER PICTOGRAPH: BARRIER CANYON, UTAH
MURAL PAINTING (RESTORED): AWATOVI, ARIZONA

The Basketmakers, challenged by blank sandstone canyon walls, responded with paintings of tall, square-shouldered figures, or with etchings that showed details of costumes. When Pueblo builders began to finish the walls of their kivas and houses with plaster, a thousand years ago, they had an ideal surface for mural paintings; these show figures whose masks and costumes are like those used in Pueblo rituals even today.

FROM MASKS TO MODELING

The making of masks, idols, and ceramic funeralware was widespread in the Americas. To the Indian, the wearer of a mask became what the mask represented, and so took on magic powers. Masks were used in hunting and in rites to bring good hunting and other necessities of life.

DEER MASK: KEY MARCO, FLORIDA

The wooden deer mask shown here was made by now-extinct Calusa Indians of Florida. The hinged ears could be moved by means of strings, giving a lifelike appearance to the performance of the wearer.

IROQUOIS CORNHUSK MASK

Wooden masks, characterized by distortion of human features, were most generally used by the Indians of the northeastern United States area. This mask, of braided and fringed cornhusks, was distinctive with the Iroquois Husk Face Society and was worn during the curing rites when offerings were made to tribal spirits in propitiation or thanksgiving.

SPIRIT MASK: ALASKA

Unlike the realistic doe mask from Florida, the Eskimo seal mask does not show a natural form but rather the seal spirit, as imagined by the maker. Other masks depart from reality altogether and depict spirits thought to live in lonely places and to bring misfortune to men. By dreaming of these spirits, in visions brought on by fasting and torture, the medicine men hoped to gain the power of the spirits. Masks representing the spirits were thought to turn the wearers into beings with such power that they could heal the sick, bring good hunting, and exert other magic influences.

KACHINAS OF THE HOPI INDIANS: ARIZONA

Elkskin masks like the one in the drawing on page 104 are still worn by modern Zuñi Indians in their tribal dances. The character represented is one of the gods thought to come to Zuñi villages around the first of December to bless new households. Kachina dolls represented the masked figures who took part in such ritual ceremonies. The masked dancers served in child training, by appearing at due intervals to warn or punish children. If these "bogey-men" would not frighten children into being good, what would?

MOCHICA PORTRAIT VESSEL: CHICAMAC VALLEY, PERU

EARLY CHIMU PORTRAIT VESSEL: PERU

The making of pottery figures and of portrait vases reached an amazing level of skill among Indians of the Peruvian coastal desert several centuries after Christ. These ceramics, made to be put into the graves of rulers, are so skillfully fashioned that they reach beyond the craft of pottery making into the art of sculpture.

MAIZE GOD: COPÁN, HONDURAS

This sculptured limestone head from Copán is the finest known example of
a type of sculpture found in early Mayan cities in Honduras and Guatemala.
These figures, made in about the eighth century A.D., are called "maize gods."
They appeared on the façades of temples such as that on page 32. A crest of
curling corn leaves crowns the heads. Mask-pendants and earplugs were
probably copied from jade ornaments worn by priests. The extended hands
suggest the gesture of a life-giving god, who may be dropping the grains of
corn into the ground and blessing them.

SEATED CLAY FIGURE: CENTRAL VERACRUZ, MEXICO

The sculptor who made this clay statue was surely enjoying himself. The pose is even more relaxed than that of the Mayan astronomer and has none of the solemn beauty and dignity of the Maize God. This individual may have dropped down for a moment's rest during a dance or ceremony.

The artists who modeled or carved these figures of clay or stone were as creative, as religious, and as skillful as were the Europeans of their day. Theirs was the first great American art, and it was an achievement worth our study and highest appreciation.

MAYA ASTRONOMER: CHIAPAS, MEXICO

The figure of a Mayan astronomer seated on a calendar hieroglyph is a small statuette nine inches high which Dr. Spinden dates two or three centuries after the greatest Mayan period. The modeling is free, as if the sculptor were enjoying a personal style not permitted in the religious art of earlier days. The figure may wear a mask.

METALWORK

GOLD STAFF HEAD: COLOMBIA   GOLD FEMALE FIGURE: COLOMBIA

Although it is generally considered that at the time of Columbus Indians were in the Stone Age because they used stone weapons and tools, certain groups were very skillful workers in precious metals. Mochican-Chimu gold-workers were as good at modeling as were the pottery makers. Colombian tribes made remarkable gold sculptures of gods and animals. Peruvian rulers had palaces lined with golden objects, and gardens full of lifelike golden and silver flowers. Millions of dollars' worth of such treasures were melted down by European rulers. European goldsmiths were amazed at the wonderful workmanship shown in these pieces, but the objects they described have long since disappeared. It was the gold, not the art, that the white conquerors worshiped.

ARCHITECTURE OF THE UNITED STATES AREA

The Indian had not really got under way as a builder in the United States area at the time of the Discovery. The simple wood and thatch structures of the northern regions soon disappeared. In the southwestern semidesert, however, sun-hardened adobe brick and stone block buildings remain from a thousand years ago.

PUEBLO BONITO: CHACO CANYON, NEW MEXICO

After the arrival of corn culture from Mexico, communal apartment-house pueblos sprang up. Pueblo Bonito was one of twelve built in Chaco Canyon, New Mexico, at about the time of the Mound Builders and the Vikings, as is shown by tree beams dating from 919 to 1130 A.D. A severe drought caused the final abandonment of this and other settlements. Pueblo Bonito was built in the form of a "D," the straight front a double row of single-story rooms opening into an enclosed central plaza. It rose to five and six stories with a forty-foot wall at the back and a single narrow entrance.

PREHISTORIC CLIFF DWELLINGS: MESA VERDE, COLORADO

These dwellings, built in a cavern on a mesa eight thousand feet above sea level, presumably during the twelfth century, show great skill in planning and construction. Many of the numerous rooms have fireplaces, and some have frescoes decorating the interior walls.

29

TAOS PUEBLO: NEW MEXICO

Taos is a several-storied adobe community house where Indian life goes on today much as it did in ancient times. Walpi, Acoma, and Zuñi are other mesa pueblos still occupied.

The wooden temples that may have crowned the earth ramps of the Mound Builders have disappeared. A round earth lodge found near Macon, Georgia, contained an eagle effigy altar very like that found in a similar round structure in Mexico. Strong evidences of Mexica-Mayan influences exist in the United States area, as we have seen, but the puzzle of migrations has not yet been fully solved.

TEMPLE BASE: UAXACTÚN, GUATEMALA

The greatest development of Indian architecture began with the Mayas almost two thousand years ago. This small, plastered temple base had already been buried underneath a later structure before the stela with a date corresponding to 328 A.D. was erected here. By this date the people of northern Europe and England, though no longer barbaric tribes, had little architecture beyond that of their Roman conquerors. The Mayan Indians, however, at this time had developed astronomy, writing, arithmetic, a calendar, and were well started on a great architectural development.

This temple base contained in capsule form the style of architecture which in the next thousand years was to flower in amazingly beautiful temples and palaces built almost all over Central America. This pyramid base, the stairways broken by stone masks, the altar on the flat top—all were to be repeated hundreds of times during ten centuries.

Uaxactún and other Mayan sacred centers of Guatemala and Honduras flourished from the first to the seventh centuries A.D. These towns were built by tribes with a language, art, and architecture in common, and a civilization based on corn culture. The "cities" were sacred centers where the temples to the gods were built, as well as the palaces of priests and rulers whose duty it was to serve the gods of earth and sky upon whom the corn crop depended.

MODEL OF RUINS: COPÁN, HONDURAS

These sacred centers were well planned. In this model we see a part of Copán, showing features usual in Mayan centers: an open plaza with staircase ramps, the Hieroglyphic Stairway (see opposite page), the great Ball Court, with staircase ramps up either side for spectators, the Reviewing Stand, and the temple with the sculptured doorway, where the Maize God (page 25) was a feature of architectural decoration.

HIEROGLYPHIC STAIRWAY: COPÁN, HONDURAS

The Hieroglyphic Stairway, dated 770 A.D., has ninety steps, each a foot high and carved with hieroglyphs, making in all a giant page of Mayan writing. Many other Mayan temples used ninety steps on four sides, giving the sacred number, three hundred and sixty—that of the days in the Mayan calendar year. Each group of twelve steps of this stairway is marked off by a carved stone figure. All of this stonework was done without metal tools.

From the façade of the temple of the Sculptured Doorway, the Maize God looked down on the city of Copán.

TEMPLE OF THE CROSS (MODEL): PALENQUE, MEXICO

At Palenque, in southern Mexico, the Mayas built a temple group of great beauty along a tropical hillside stream. The roof-comb of the temple shown here was made by the meeting of two slanting walls, carved with lacelike delicacy. We show a model of this temple as it probably looked a thousand years ago. You must imagine the brilliant colors which the tropical sun and rain have long since stripped from its stones. Here at Palenque, it has been said, the Mayan gods were not heavy and severe but were beings of an "elegant aristocracy."

The greatest number of Mayan building dates, says Dr. Spinden, fell around 790 A.D. Dated stelae were set up for another century, after which these early Mayan centers were abandoned. Mayan art styles, however, traveled outward with the Mayas, who migrated in search of new corn land.

34

MEXICA-MAYAN ARCHITECTURE

During the ninth century, architecture began to develop farther north in Mexico, among the Toltecs. The valley of Mexico was, from ice-age days, a vast arena where various tribes engaged in struggles dimly remembered in legends and shown in ceramics and art forms. The Toltecs came in before 700 A.D. and built a number of sacred centers, of which the most remarkable was Teotihuacán, "Where the Gods Reside."

PYRAMID OF THE SUN: TEOTIHUACÁN, MEXICO

The so-called Temple of the Sun is an enormous pyramid of basaltic lava and adobe. It is two hundred and sixteen feet high, covers over ten acres, and its base is seven hundred and twenty feet by seven hundred and sixty feet. The great stairway leads up to a flat top where an altar structure once was and where there stood, according to legend, a colossal image of the Sun deity, wearing gold and silver breastplates that reflected the rising sun.

The Toltecs did not bring this pyramidal style from the north, where underground kivas were usual, but when we look at the early Mayan temples, we see that this enormous pyramid is an expanded form of the Mayan temple base.

TEMPLE OF QUETZALCOATL:
TEOTIHUACÁN, MEXICO

This structure still shows the brilliant paint upon its serpent masks. It owes its protection from despoliation to the fact that it had been buried to form a base for a later temple, a process the Toltecs repeated every fifty-two years.

TEMPLE BASE: XOCHICALCO, MEXICO

A similar Toltec temple, an hour's drive from Mexico City, is dated around
the middle of the tenth century. Here the Plumed Serpent alternated with
glyphs said to be those of the Zapotecs. The human figures in this pyramid
are clearly in the Mayan style.

INNER COURT OF A PALACE: MITLA, MEXICO

In a fertile valley, in what is now the state of Oaxaca, a group of exquisite palace buildings mark the place where, according to legend, a great high priest once lived. The Zapotec name Mictlín means "Place of Beatitudes," which suggests the presence of priests of great power. The great rooms in these palace buildings are like audience chambers. Mitla tombs, though plundered for centuries, have recently given up treasures of gold and silver ornaments. These ruins are of the period around 1200 and 1300 A.D. and represent a peak of architectural skill of which any race might be proud.

The delicacy of the stonework is shown in this view of an interior court. Like a jigsaw puzzle, each piece of stone in this fretwork was carved to fit into a particular place, and each locked in place at the back. A foremost archaeologist estimates that some eighty thousand carved pieces were used for the wall of one inner court alone. The over-all effect of walls painted in many colors and softened by cloth hangings at doors must have been of impressive brilliance.

PALACE OF THE NUNS: UXMAL, MEXICO

Early Mayan settlers are said to have reached Uxmal, in Mexico, in the sixth century, and Toltec chieftains came later. The "nunnery" shown here was so named by Spanish conquerors because its ninety cell-like rooms seemed like a convent and its lacy stone carving like lacework done by Spanish nuns. This building was on a platform some fifteen feet high, as was customary in this center. The court surrounded by its group of four palaces was two hundred and fifty-eight feet long.

MAYAN TEMPLE, "RIO BEC. B": QUINTANA ROO, MEXICO

This ancient ruin in southern Mexico looks somewhat like the two-towered churches that Indians were to build all over Central America under the direction of Spanish priests. Look carefully, however, and you will see the germ of the early Mayan temple base in this eighth- or ninth-century structure. Each tower is copied from the pyramidal temple base, but terraces have become mere ledges, and the stairway a meaningless decoration so steep that even a monkey could not climb it. Towers are pure decoration, with no altar room inside. Roof-combs are still used but have become useless stone trellises. Masks and human figures appear but have no distinction. The men who built

MODEL OF "RIO BEC. B"

this structure of limestone blocks were skillful builders, for the two sides of this eighty-four-foot ruin vary only an inch in length, but they were no longer great architects working in a living style in which every part of the building served a function.

This ruin had a curious history. It was carefully studied by a Peabody Museum expedition in 1912, as was another ruin, called Rio Bec. A, only a quarter of a mile away. A later expedition relocated Rio Bec. A, but the jungle had swallowed up Rio Bec. B, and searchers working in the area where it had been reported to be were unable to locate it again.

TEMPLE OF THE FRESCOES: TULUM, MEXICO

A late Mayan seacoast city, Tulum, is built within walls, a custom never followed by the early Mayas. Within the walls of Tulum are fifty-four ruins. Many others lie beyond. This small temple reminds us of the altar temples atop earlier Mayan pyramids. It was rebuilt several times, the upper rooms being a later addition.

42

MODEL OF THE TEMPLE OF THE FRESCOES

This vivid restoration is a splendid example of the work done by archaeologists in reconstructing the original appearance of ancient Indian buildings. Precision and skill in calculating complete measurements and proportions on the basis of those of the existing structure, and extreme patience and expertness in fitting together the bits and pieces of the available remaining ornamentation, combine to reproduce here the striking beauty of Mayan architecture.

TEMPLE OF THE THREE LINTELS: CHICHEN ITZÁ, MEXICO

Chichen Itzá was one of the great religious centers of Yucatán for hundreds of years. The Temple of the Three Lintels, in the older part of the city, is a charming little palace on a low platform. Three doors lead into three separate rooms. A serpent motif runs in a band around the lintel. Masks ornament the corners.

44

CARACOL OR OBSERVATORY: CHICHEN ITZÁ, MEXICO

This round building, Caracol, was named by the Spanish conquerors, who thought its inner spiral stairway resembled the shell of a snail.

It probably served some purpose in the ritual of worship of the Wind or Creator God, Kukulcan (or Quetzalcoatl, the Mexican Plumed Serpent God). Upper windows were so placed that they marked the rising point of certain planets at the spring and autumn equinoxes.

EL CASTILLO: CHICHEN ITZÁ, MEXICO

El Castillo, the Castle, is the Spanish name for another temple to Kukulcan, guarding the way to the Sacred *Cenote*. Four staircases with ninety steps each make up the sacred number of calendar days. Nine terraces, two on either side of each staircase, make the eighteen months. This temple, built a thousand years after the pre-Mayan temple with which we opened this story of Mayan building, is, as you can see, merely a larger and more magnificent version of the same idea. Who can say when and where a third Mayan period might have arisen had the white men not arrived to plunder, enslave, and all but destroy the Mayas?

46

INCA ARCHITECTURE

By comparison with Mayan architecture, that of the Incas, with its solid block masonry and massive regularity of form, appears heavy and severe. Actually, however, while the Inca buildings lack the variety and romantic quality of the best of the Mayan structures, they present an interesting parallel with modern "functional" architecture, to the extent that their designs conform to the particular purpose for which each was intended.

MACHU PICCHU: PERU (GENERAL VIEW)

This is an ancient and secret Inca town which was never discovered by the Spanish explorers. Hidden high on a mountain above tremendous gorges, this hillside center may have sheltered the sacred nuns and the remnant of the Inca court which escaped the Spaniards. In its graveyards hundreds of skeletons of girls, women, and boys have been found, but none of grown men.

47

STREET IN CUZCO, SHOWING INCA MASONRY: PERU

Here is a superb example of the magnificent "dry-stone" construction of Inca walls and buildings. No one knows the precise methods by which these stones were cut and shaped to fit together so firmly that they remain, after centuries, as evidence of the engineering genius of their builders.

AMERICANS BEFORE COLUMBUS

I. THE FIRST AMERICANS

Carib Song[*]

I am the force of the spirit of the lightning eel, the thunder axe, the
　　stone.
I am the force of the firefly, thunder and lightning I have created.

The Caribs were a savage tribe not typical of pre-Columbian Indians.
This song is to their storm god, a serpent symbol like the Chinese
thunder dragon of rainstorms. This widespread ancient symbol is common to the American Indians and many Asiatic peoples.

[*] Sources of poems quoted in this book will be found on pp. 265—66

THE FIRST AMERICANS

WHEN a red-haired boy baby, born in Genoa in about 1450, was christened Cristoforo Colombo, there is no record that a fairy godmother stood beside his crib to promise him the wealth of the Indies. It would have been a promise well worth recording. For several hundred years, the merchants of Genoa and Venice and other ports of what we now call Italy had been piling up wealth through their trade in the treasures of the Indies: jewels, silks, rugs, spices, perfumes, and dyes. These merchants shipped the products of Europe to the Levantine ports on the eastern shores of the Mediterranean, to trade them for these treasures that had been brought overland across Asia. Or they sailed to

51

Egypt, in whose markets they found the silks and spices that had reached Egypt by way of the Indian Ocean and the Red Sea. In either case, the wealth of the Indies reached them after passing through many hands. How much more wealthy the merchant of Europe might become who could discover a route by which he might sail his ships directly to the fabulous Indies!

By 1476 the red-haired baby had become a young man who one day found himself in a very dangerous place: in a sea battle with the French, the Genoese ships were rammed and set afire. Jumping from his flaming ship into the sea, Cristoforo Colombo was lucky enough to find an oar to which he clung and so was able to reach the shore. It was the shore of Portugal, the land from which Prince Henry the Navigator had sent forth his ships to find the Indies. It seemed a good omen, for this was a young man with one particular dream: the dream that by sailing west across the Ocean Sea, one might reach the East. To most of the people of his day, who could see for themselves that the earth was flat, this was a crazy dream. But certain learned men of the past had believed, as this man did, that the world was round.

Christopher Columbus, as we call him, was not the only man of his day who thought that the earth was round, but perhaps he believed more strongly than others did that it was his own destiny to cross the Ocean Sea. For many years he tried to interest the rulers of Portugal, and then of Spain, but no one would give him the ships he needed. If the rulers were dubious about risking their wealth, so were the sailors fearful about risking their necks in such a wild venture. The Sea of Darkness was a fearful thing to think about. Sailing south, into the heat of the sun, one would burn to a crisp; even the ocean boiled! Then there was the Sargasso Sea, where ships stuck forever in the seaweed. And there were monsters that speared the ship and held it in the air, and others, like the giant squid, that encircled it with slimy arms and drew it under the water. And what if the ship passed through these dangers, what then? It would only reach the edge of the world and fall off into nothingness!

COLUMBUS CAME LATE. The long story of Christopher Columbus has been told many times. It reached its high note of triumph on October 12, 1492, the date perhaps best known to young Americans. This is the day we keep in celebration of the discovery of America. But America had been discovered a great many times before 1492. Columbus came very late: what about the people who came down to the shore to meet his ships?

When Columbus set the Spanish standard into the sand of the island that he named San Salvador, he thought that he had sailed around the world and had reached the Indies. That is why he called the copper-skinned men he found there "Indians." These were not, of course, the people of India. They were the original Americans. The sailor had discovered a new world, not that old one for which he was looking.

Men had lived in the Americas many thousands of years before Columbus discovered the New World. This period of time we call pre-Columbian. Some of the people of pre-Columbian America were uncivilized hunters who wandered after the herds of wild game. Others lived in simple villages and tended cornfields. Still others lived in cities as amazingly beautiful as any in the Old World, cities in which the arts, crafts, religious ceremonies, and forms of government were highly developed. The people of pre-Columbian America spoke many languages. Their customs and religious and political systems differed widely. Their story is wonderful and tragic. Much of it has doubtless been lost forever.

The ancestors of these people had themselves once discovered America, for man is not native to our hemisphere. First of all, let us set the stage for their appearance. You may wonder how such an ancient story became known: the answer is that the earth itself kept the record throughout long ages until man became intelligent enough to read it. Hills and valleys and rocks and the bones of men and animals are the books from which we learn the story of America's prehistoric past.

ICE-AGE AMERICA. Though man himself was a late-comer to our hemisphere, horses and camels and dogs and many other animals come from families that were really and truly American, in that they had developed here during the sixty or so millions of years since the dinosaurs died away and gave the meek and lowly mammals a chance to inherit the earth. For many ages these animal families had found the Americas a happy hunting ground. Then, about a million years ago, a strange and uncomfortable change in climate began to make life difficult for them. Winters grew colder and more snow stayed on the ground each year. Mountains of ice formed in the north and slowly advanced southward, driving the animals before them. Ice sheets piled up a mile thick over New England and thousands of feet deep in the northern part of the Mississippi valley. Four times in the long geological age called the Pleistocene epoch, the ice periods came and went. In between the glacial ages there were warm periods during which animals and plants spread northward again from their cold-weather retreats in California, Florida, and other southern areas.

These ice-age animal resorts were like an enormous circus, one which was never viewed by human eyes. Their story may be read in such places as the tar pits of the Rancho La Brea, near Los Angeles. During Pleistocene days, a natural tar trap was formed there, at a place where petroleum oozed up from oil-bearing rock strata fractured by an earthquake. Rain stood upon the surface of these tar pools to form what looked like natural lakes. Over a period of centuries, many thousands of animals were trapped in the tar.

A giant sloth might blunder into the pool and find the tar sinking beneath his feet. A saber-toothed tiger in search of his dinner would leap to the back of the sloth, only to have his own feet caught in the sticky tar. Giant condors circling overhead would drop down to feed upon the dying animals and would themselves become trapped. Migratory birds would settle upon the innocent-looking lake of death, to rise no more. Even a peacock strayed there, far from his Asiatic home.

Thousands of fossils of animals long extinct in the Americas are found in the Rancho La Brea tar bed. Among them are elephants, bison, lions, wolves, horses, and camels.

The variety of animals whose bones are found at La Brea tells us of a most amazing reshuffling of the world's animal population which began about a million years ago and continued until the end of the last ice age. Horses and camels had been native to America and had spread to Europe and Asia at times when the great land masses were joined by a narrow bridge of land or ice across the Bering Strait, where the two continents almost meet.

The horses, a purely American family, some species of which were larger than the draft horses of today, became world travelers. Some pushed down through the Panama gateway into South America. Others crossed into Asia by means of the Bering road-way, there to escape the mysterious fate which destroyed the entire horse population of the two Americas some ten thousand years ago.

The camels also traveled both to Asia and to South America, where their small modern cousins, the llamas, still lived on after the larger forms had died out in the Americas. Meanwhile mammoths and mastodons had crossed the Siberian wastes to reach North America, where they flourished until they, too, mysteriously became extinct. The giant sloths and the enormous, armadillo-like glyptodonts came to North America fairly recently from Central and South America, after the Isthmus of Panama had risen to form a land bridge between the long-separated American continents.

As these large game animals made their slow way across the Bering bridge, unluckily for themselves they lured into the New

World the most dangerous carnivore that has ever stalked the earth. This was man—the only creature that has ever learned how to make fire and to chip weapons and tools of stone.

With fire and chipped stone spear points and little else, the first men entered the Americas. Even the greatest boaster of this race of hunters could never have foretold how quickly man's appearance would be followed by the extinction of some forty million game animals of Pleistocene America. Let us take a look at this new and ferocious American arrival. Our imaginary scene takes place on the ledge of a cliff in the southwestern part of North America, perhaps twenty thousand years ago.

ICE-AGE AMERICANS. It was a damp, drizzly day, with a cold northern wind blowing southward from the mountains of ice to the north.

Several children stood on the ledge in front of a cave dug in a limestone cliff. Before them stretched a wide valley in which lay a chain of lakes, and beyond that was the smoky plume of a volcano.

Behind them in the large cave, several people were at work. A young woman scraped the flesh from a bison hide which she had pegged down upon the ground before her. A man was sitting by the fire, shaping a flint spearhead by means of another sharp stone. The women wore aprons of tanned bison hide and the man a loincloth made of a bit of hide. They all looked very much alike, with brown skins, slanting black eyes, and a tangle of straight black hair.

Around the fire on the cave floor was an untidy litter of the broken bones of horses and camels, the tusks of mammoths and mastodons, and bits of flint. Farther back were piles of animal skins used as beds.

The children on the ledge were watching a herd of bison grazing below in the valley. Now the powerful leader of the herd raised his shaggy head to sniff the wind, but he did not see what was clearly visible to the watchers from the ledge—a half-circle of hunters creeping forward under cover of the underbrush, their spears balanced in their hands.

Then suddenly everything happened at once. The hunters sprang from behind the bushes and leveled their spears at the herd of bison. The whoops of the hunters, the roars of charging bison, the squeals of calves and cows as they tried to escape— all this distant noise went to the heads of the children on the ledge, who tumbled down the slope of the cliff and ran to join their fathers and older brothers.

In a babble of boasting and laughter the hunters began to skin the animals they had killed. Now and then someone would pause to hack off a juicy-looking steak and carry it back to roast over the campfire, but much of the meat was left to be eaten by animals and birds of prey. These hunters were interested in hides rather than in meat. Hides were useful for a variety of purposes: they could be worn as aprons or wraps or hung in the doorways. And when they were laid on the cave floor, their furry softness was a great improvement on cold stone or damp earth. With their edges held or tied together, hides served to carry roots and fruits, or they could be used as water bags. Sometimes babies rode in hides slung over their mothers' shoulders.

On the night of which we are telling, there were singing and rejoicing in the cave. The older hunters repeated for the hundredth time the stories of their remarkable victories over tiger, mammoth, or cave bear. They recounted how they speared or trapped the big animals and how, in the dry season, they would set fire to grasses and force whole herds of horses or mammoths over the edge of a cliff.

Wide-eyed, the children listened as they played in the flickering shadows beyond their mothers' backs. Naturally they could not know that as the climate changed and this rich southwestern land dried to a semidesert, time and change—aided by man the hunter —were to destroy millions of the game animals that made the Americas a happy hunting ground.

The early Americans whom we have just described were not like ourselves in skin and hair coloring, for they belonged to a different race. They had not come from Europe, where some of our own ancestors at this time, the tall and artistic Cro-Magnon men who had taken Europe away from the ungainly Neanderthals, were painting bison, mammoths, and horses on Spanish and French cave walls while our first American hunters were pursuing the same kinds of animals across the American plains.

Yet if we were to see one of the early American hunters in a crowd today, provided that he had a modern suit of clothes and a haircut, we should not run away shrieking. He would look much like our American Indians, with his copper-colored skin, straight black hair, and slanting black eyes. These characteristics identify his family group, the Mongoloid branch of mankind, whose original home was Central Asia.

How Man Reached the Americas. It is only recently that

scientists have known how these earliest Americans looked or even how they reached America. There have been many theories about the origin of the people to whom Columbus gave the confusing name "Indians" at a time when he still thought that he had discovered the short route to India.

Before the scientific study of ancient bones and stones long hidden in the earth had made the true story clear, people imagined that there had been a long-vanished race from whom the Indians of Central and South America had learned the skills to construct the wonderful temples which the white man found there. According to legend, this highly civilized race lived on a great island called Atlantis, which "in a night and a day, with thunders and fury of winds" sank beneath the Atlantic Ocean, carrying its whole history into oblivion.

It has also been suggested that the Americas may have been settled by a people from a legendary island supposed to have been in the Pacific. Mu, like Atlantis, is a myth, though in each case some real happening may be symbolized in the story. It is quite likely, however, that islanders who at one time made immense voyages over a wide area in the Pacific in their outrigger canoes may indeed have reached the coasts of South America. In the same way, mariners from Asia and from Europe may have been blown to American shores.

Interesting though these speculations are, today every scientist agrees that the Indian race reached America from Asia by means of the Bering Strait, in a long series of migrations that took place from time to time over thousands of years, and that the Indian arts and crafts were "made in America."

The true story is even more wonderful than the legends because it is real. It is a story of epic size, of ordinary human beings faced with the challenge of the unknown and dangerous, and of the courage and endurance with which these men, women, and children traveled by foot across the icy top of the world, to leave

Asia behind them and cross the Bering Strait to America. As time passed, they found their way down the cold northland into the endless Great Plains, from which they spread by countless ways. Some of the groups settled here and there along the way. Others pushed on across high mountains and through danger-infested jungles until, perhaps many centuries after the first arrival in America, people had reached the southern tip of the Americas, the cold land strangely named Tierra del Fuego, or "Land of Fire." In the following chapter we will examine some of the clues they left behind them as they passed, in restless generations, across the face of the Americas.

II. THE HUNTERS
AND THE HUNTED

With Dangling Hands

Come all game animals large,
Come all game animals small,
Hither come with dangling hands
To Nambe town! So now come all
To Nambe town with dangling hands!

This magic-making song asks the game animals to come and be slain, since to "come with dangling hands" would be to come home over the hunter's shoulder. By creating such a mental picture, primitive man hoped to bring about the events for which he prayed.

Magic hunting songs, the first poetry, were common among aboriginal tribes.

THE HUNTERS AND THE HUNTED

O NCE the small bands of hunters had crossed over the Bering
Strait into America, with the cold winds from off the icecaps
blowing on their backs, they wandered southward toward the sun,
following the game animals. The men carried their spears, the
women strapped their babies on their backs, and children and
puppies scrambled along as best they could. For the most part,
the trail of these ancient Americans has vanished as completely
as has the smoke of their campfires, but now and then modern
scientists unearth traces of their passing.

Such traces give us evidence of several main groups of hunters who are known to have lived here ten and even twenty thousand years ago. Their story was very hard to puzzle out because they were constantly moving back and forth, and they left little behind them except a few stone weapons.

You might picture America as an enormous tourist camp where for over two hundred centuries various hunting tribes came and went, leaving behind them castoff tools and weapons and the bones of the animals they ate. Winds and streams deposited dust and sand over this litter, in time building up solid earth many feet deep above the ancient camp sites. Centuries later, wind and water tore away the earth covering here and there and left a stone spear point, lost two hundred centuries ago, beside an arrowhead hardly more ancient than your own great-grandfather.

Yet a scientist trained in Indian anthropology can tell a spear point made twenty thousand years ago from a point made thousands of years later almost as easily as you can tell a jeep from a Ford. He can tell you what part of the country a bit of Indian pottery came from and how many centuries ago it was made. You may wonder how such objects can be dated.

Archaeologists have learned the order in which the Indian tools and other objects were made by studying the earth layers in which they were found. In certain caves and sheltered places the soil has lain undisturbed by erosion or plow for the thousands of years since the first Americans lived there, dropping gnawed bones of animals and throwing away broken tools and weapons. Floods have washed sand over cave floors, and winds have blown dust that settled thickly over everything. In this way more and more layers of earth have been built up. Anthropologists cannot guess where man's early camp sites may lie buried in open country, but they can dig down to the rock bottom of a cave and can sift out every object left there by early man. These objects may be roughly dated by means of the layers of sand, clay, or "cave stone" (a rock-like crust formed by water dripping from the cave roof), in which the objects are found. These layers tell of cold, wet ice-age periods followed by warmer and dryer times when ice sheets were in retreat. In general, scientists know when these changes occurred.

Even in the open country, it has sometimes happened that wind and rain, and streams cutting through layers of earth built up through thousands of years, have uncovered bones or chipped stone objects that showed the scientists where to dig for other stories of America's most ancient men. Such bones or tools have been found almost everywhere in the Americas.

ANCIENT MEN IN SOUTH AMERICA. The trail of bones and artifacts (as the weapons and stones are called) leads from North America down the Mexican plateau and across the Isthmus of Panama into South America. Some of the clues are very old indeed. In the valley of Mexico, for example, human bones have been found underneath ancient lava flows. In Nicaragua, bison bones and human footprints are found together in rock that was once soft volcanic mud. In Ecuador and elsewhere, traces of man have been found with the bones of long-extinct animals.

When you look at a map of the American continents with their plateaus, rivers, and jungles, it seems as if such a journey must have taken hundreds of years, and it probably did. The tribes could travel no faster than children and women burdened with babies could walk. Yet it has been said that if a group had moved camp about three miles southward each week, a baby carried across the ice floe at Bering Strait might have lived to reach the southern tip of South America.

No one knows how long it actually took the first Americans to cross the high, bare crags of the Andes mountains or to thread their way through the hot, perilous swamps of the enormous Amazon valley. Yet at least ten thousand years ago, human families were living in a cave in Minas Geraes, Brazil, where they gnawed and threw away the bones of the now-extinct animals they hunted. One of them died in the cave, and during the next

several thousand years the waters of Lake Confins laid down silt above his body, providing scientists with a method of judging how long ago he lived. Bones and tools have also been found in Argentina, Chile, and other parts of South America.

Among the most ancient human remains that can be dated are several skeletons found in Patagonia, at the level of the original rock floor of a cave. The dust of five thousand years had settled down in undisturbed earth layers above these bones. Like most of the early men in America, these early Patagonian people had long, rather than round, heads, the "shovel-shaped" upper incisor teeth common to Mongolians and to American Indians, and certain other characteristics found among the people of Asia.

Scientific studies of these and many thousands of other skulls, found along the Bering route and elsewhere, show that the ancestors of the earliest American Indians came of a Mongoloid stock occasionally showing traces of an early white Asiatic strain.

"MINNESOTA MAN." One skeleton showing these mixed human strains has become famous under the name of "Minnesota Man"

—or, as joking students call it, "Minnesota Minnie," since the skeleton is that of a girl.

Unfortunately the scientists are not always present when ancient bones are discovered, and so cannot be sure that the earth layers above them are undisturbed. Such was the case with "Minnesota Man." This fossil skeleton was found by a road-building crew excavating twelve feet of solid Minnesota clay in 1932. When the road boss saw the bones, he stopped the big earth-moving machine and carefully uncovered the skeleton with smaller hand tools in the presence of witnesses who later testified that the earth layers above the bones lay unbroken. Studying the earth and the bones, anthropologist A. E. Jenks concluded that this ancient American girl had perished in Pelican Lake, a glacial lake which existed in Minnesota near the end of the last ice age. Probably plunging through thin ice to drown in the lake, this unlucky girl's body was gradually covered by sand and clay dropped by the lake water. The silt showed bands of dark and light, laid down by the winter and summer deposits of fifteen or twenty thousand years. Witnesses thought there was no break in the earth layers above the bones, as would have been the case if the body had been buried.

A study of the skeleton showed it to be that of a girl of about fifteen years. From the evidence of her teeth and skull, this girl was Mongoloid, with traces of an early white strain. She probably looked somewhat like a Sioux Indian. You would not have considered her pretty: her jaws and teeth stuck out, her nose was snub and her forehead low and receding. Perhaps she was not considered attractive even in her own day. Scientists studying her skull have suggested that she was hit on the head and pushed into the water.

Just as modern girls collect a variety of things in their purses, the Minnesota girl cherished magic-making objects: the bones of a bird's foot, a loon leg, and a tooth. She carried this Stone Age medicine kit in a container of turtle shell. Not putting her entire faith in magic, she also carried a dagger made of elk antler, which she probably wore around her neck on a leather string which was passed through a hole in the dagger handle. To the sorrow of anthropologists, she did not carry spear points or perish in company with an animal known to have become extinct at a certain time. However, she did wear a pendant made from a conch shell from the waters of the Gulf of Mexico. This shows that there may have been trade between her tribe and others scattered from Minnesota to the Gulf.

Not every anthropologist agrees that "Minnesota Minnie" was the earliest known American. Some skeptics believe the skeleton to be that of a Sioux Indian given a recent burial in Pelican Lake clays. It is unfortunate that these critics were not present when the bones were dug up and therefore could not be sure they had lain undisturbed in the layers of earth. It is unfortunate, also, that two other recent finds in Minnesota are subject to the same doubt. Unless Americans learn to put down their tools and telegraph for a trained anthropologist at the first glimpse of what may be a very old human skeleton, more evidence of man's early occupation of the Americas will be lost.

Sandia Man and Folsom Man. Flint spear points found in New Mexico tell us of at least two ancient human invasions of our country. The earliest was that of "Sandia Man," who may have lived over twenty thousand years ago. The story of Sandia Man comes from the finding of chipped-stone weapons, together with the charred and gnawed bones of horses, camels, sloths, and other long-extinct American animals, in the Sandia Mountains of New Mexico.

This discovery was made in 1936 by anthropologists who were searching for more evidence of the already known Folsom Man, whose spear points were first found in Folsom, New Mexico, and later were discovered to be widely distributed over the United

States. In 1936 these Folsom people were known only by their spear points; not so much as a bone or a tooth had been found to show what they were like, and no trace of them had been discovered in earth layers that had accumulated over some twelve thousand years.

Searching the earth for an answer to their questions about Folsom Man, anthropologists crawled into a dusty cave in the Sandia Mountains and sifted the earth of the cave floor. Below the recent layers they found a hard crust of cave stone and, underneath that, another dry-weather layer, in which they discovered flint lance points which were clearly those of the Folsom hunters, along with the bones of saber-toothed tigers, mammoths, camels, bison, and giant sloths.

Below this layer of rubbish left by careless Folsom housekeepers, the scientists found yet another wet-weather layer, telling the story of an earlier time when cold winds from northern glaciers reached even the warm Southwest. In this ancient layer of earth, which geologists estimated to be twenty-five thousand years old, they found more bones and more spear points.

The sterile layer of earth which was laid down in the Sandia cave after Sandia Man had lived there, and again much later after Folsom Man had disappeared, speaks of cold and dripping ages when even this sheltered southwestern cave was uninhabitable to man. Like the animals upon which they fed, these two races of ancient American hunters seem to have vanished from their old hunting grounds.

Yuma Men and Later Hunters. The ill winds that blew away some twenty feet of soil during the terrible drought years in the middle 1930's blew good luck to archaeologists. By digging into the fine sand deposits above the ice-age lakes and streams of the Southwest, the winds revealed camp sites where the early men of the Americas had lived thousands of years ago. Streams cutting through earth layers also exposed charcoal, bones, and flint.

Evidence of still other groups of hunters has been found in Texas, in California, and in many other states. Large spear points unlike Folsom ones were found near Yuma, Colorado, and elsewhere on the Great Plains. These were sometimes eight inches long, very slender, and skillfully chipped, though they were not as delicate as Folsom points. In the Eden valley of Wyoming a rancher found so many Yuma points that he invited University of Pennsylvania scientists to investigate this site. Geologists studied the evidence given by earth layers, and paleontologists identified the bison bones found with the Yuma points, and they came to the conclusion that the men of Yuma were hunters who had lived several thousand years after Folsom Man. The bison they killed were of a modern species which had replaced Taylor's bison, the extinct breed hunted by Folsom Man.

At Abilene, Texas, other spear points were found. They had once been deeply buried in earth but were now exposed by the

cutting action of a stream. They were unlike any other spear
points found, and occurred in strata separated by many hundreds
of years. In California, also, there were ancient men; they lived
at a time when an ice-age lake covered what is now a sandy depression in the Mojave Desert.

In short, there is evidence that at different periods of time,
ranging from twenty thousand to ten thousand or so years ago,
there existed in America groups of hunters who seem later to have
mysteriously disappeared. What could have happened to these
people? Having once made the difficult journey across the north-
polar regions, they should have been able to manage to live on in
a country well stocked with game animals.

When a scientist is faced with an unsolved problem like this
one of the disappearing Sandia and Folsom hunters, what does
he do? He casts his mind about for an explanation, he searches

for additional evidence, and, if he finds none, he asks himself if there are other data which might be used to get at the answer. If the Folsom spear points appeared no more in the rock strata after 10,000 B.C., what then? What happened to the animals of the same period? To the plants? To the country itself? To the rest of the world? The answers to these questions had to come from other specialists: scientists whose work dealt with extinct animals or plants, or geological formations, or climate changes, or perhaps even with sunspots.

A study of bones found in the earth layers dating back to the days of the Sandia men and the later Folsom hunters showed that the Great Plains area had been the home of numberless species of animals. At the time the first hunters had entered the Americas, many of the native North American animal families now extinct were still in existence. Dire wolves, saber-toothed tigers, giant beavers, and innumerable other gnawers, carnivores, and browsers had flourished along with horses, camels, rhinoceroses, and other animals which are not now extinct though they died out in the Americas. These families had grown up in North America during the sixty million years following the extinction of the tyrant reptiles. But others had come here from South America by means of a land bridge now sunk except for its mountaintops, which form the islands of the Caribbean Sea. Among these animals were the tapirs, armadillos, capybaras, and the giant sloths.

THE GREAT EXTINCTION. Then, almost as suddenly as if some giant hand swept them away, a mysterious calamity fell upon the hunter and the hunted alike. The horses which grazed in tremendous herds on our western plains and on the pampas of South America disappeared completely, never to appear in the Americas again until Spanish conquerors brought them back only four centuries ago. The larger camels also disappeared, leaving only the small members of the camel family, the llamas and vicuñas of South America. The mammoth and the mastodon died out entirely, and so did the saber-toothed tiger, the dire wolf, and many other American mammals.

No one knows exactly when or why this strange "dying off" came about. No one knows how much of it to blame on man. The men who lived in Sandia cave killed these animals with their peculiar and unmistakable spear points some twenty or twenty-five thousand years ago. Then man himself no longer lived in Sandia cave, and for perhaps a hundred centuries the drip, drip, drip of ice-age moisture slowly built up a layer of cave stone that sealed down the objects he had left.

About ten thousand years later the Folsom hunters came to live in the cave, and again the bones of horse and camel, mastodon and mammoth were gnawed and flung on the cave floor. Strangely, the same thing happened again: Folsom Man himself disappeared, and for another ten thousand years the silent dust settled down in Sandia cave over the bones of now-extinct animals and the spear points of vanished hunters. You might say that perhaps it was only a landslide that blocked this cave entrance and kept men out of it, but this is not the explanation. Folsom Man had disappeared from all his old hunting grounds by about 10,000 B.C.

Who Killed Cock Robin? What strange calamity destroyed the ice-age American animals and the men who hunted them? We cannot blame the last ice-age, since horses, camels, and other Pleistocene animals also became extinct in the warm, fertile regions of Central and South America. It may be that horses and camels were destroyed by an epidemic disease such as the sleeping sickness which is caused by the tsetse fly, which makes it impossible for horses to live in certain parts of Africa today. Two species of this fly have been found in ancient rock strata in North America, and during long periods of warm, wet weather these insects could have destroyed many of the larger mammals, of which they are still the deadly enemies.

Undoubtedly lava flows and ash falls from volcanoes destroyed much plant and animal life. Herds made smaller by slaughter, drought, disease, or natural disaster may have found it hard to protect their young from animal foes, and so were unable to maintain their numbers.

We have said that man himself may have been the greatest disaster that befell the American game animals. The Folsom hunters speared scores of bison at a time, purely for their hides: we know this from a study of the skeletons of the animals they killed. But man's most destructive weapon may have been fire. By setting the dried grass alight, he may have driven hundreds of animals into ravines where they could be speared. For many years afterward, animals could not find food in such burned-over areas, and starvation would finish the destruction.

Yet it is hardly possible that the millions of animals free to roam the Americas could have been slain by man alone. It is more likely that the great herds were destroyed by the changes that came to the country itself. For when the Rocky Mountains and the Colorado plateau were pushed upward, the moist plains of the Southwest were drained and became a semiarid desert region where the great herds could not find enough food to live. The growth of thick forests along the rainy eastern seaboard was equally disastrous for the herds of grazing animals which once flourished there.

Whatever the explanation, it is clear that some crisis came to hunter and hunted alike. Something happened in this happy hunting ground where bands of nomads had lived so well that they could afford to kill the bison for the skins alone, leaving the meat uneaten.

A time of crisis is a period in which a species is judged, a time during which it struggles and manages to adapt itself to a new type of life, or, failing to do so, dies away, as the dinosaurs had done. What was the nature of the great crisis which caused the disappearance of the first Americans? Which of our guesses will prove to be the most correct? Did the first settlements of our country fail and the first human settlers die away? What questions can we ask that will be the right ones to help us solve this mystery?

III. TIME AND CHANGE

Warrior Song of the Hethu'shka Society
(OMAHA)

I shall vanish and be no more,
But the land over which I now roam
Shall remain
And change not.

This Omaha song was translated by the Omaha Indian anthropologist, Francis La Flesche, who explained that its purpose was to teach the young warrior not to think of his own safety and not to abandon those he was duty bound to protect, since death cannot be escaped.

This song was written many thousands of years after the Folsom hunters had vanished. The lands over which Folsom men had roamed had changed very greatly before the Omaha warrior made his song.

TIME AND CHANGE

Events taking place in another part of the world throw some light upon the mystery of the disappearing American hunters. During the same times that Sandia and Folsom men were meeting crises in America, other groups of hunters living in Europe from twenty to ten thousand years before Christ were having problems of their own. The men of Europe and America were hunting much the same animals: horses, camels, mammoths, and others whose bones are found in American cave dwellings also appeared in the beautiful cave drawings made by the early men of Europe. The fate of these European cave dwellers interested scientists long before anyone ever heard of a Sandia or a Folsom spear point.

Now it is known that early hunters, using stone spear points, had ranged far and wide over Africa and Europe. During the period of mountain building, changes in climate and rainfall caused these hunters to change their ways of living. Europe had been a tundra inhabited by herds of browsing animals whose ways of living were not unlike those of the caribou herds of our present northern tundras. Africa and Asia also were different from what they are today, with pleasant plains which, as ice sheets melted and moisture-carrying winds changed their courses, became deserts. The Sahara, Arabian, and Gobi deserts all preserve evidences of the early hunters who once lived there. As the grazing areas dried into deserts, the hunters had to move to other places and to live differently. In Europe, where rainfall increased, thick forests sprang up. As the Sahara became uninhabitable, some of the hunters went southward into the African jungles, where their primitive descendants may be found today. Others went east to the Nile, where, by 4000 B.C., they had learned how to farm and had founded the Egyptian civilization.

Meanwhile, as the Arabian area also became a desert, men settled down between the Tigris and Euphrates rivers to create a great civilization in the Mesopotamian valley. As people became more dependent on grains and fruits, they began to plant and protect such crops. Swamps were drained, crops sown and protected, and houses built. In short, men became town dwellers.

The same thing happened somewhat later in the rich river valleys of India, where the human race may first have developed half a million or more years earlier. Several thousand years before the birth of Christ, the Chinese were beginning to plant rice in the marshes of the Yellow River.

Thus little farming communities began to spring up along the banks of the rivers of the Old World. There men learned that plants will produce food if they are watered and tended, and that animals who come to drink and feed may be tamed. For although savages sometimes adopt baby animals as pets, the taming of animals probably came about when water holes and food plants were scarce and the herds were half starved. Then, driven by hunger, they probably invaded the grain patches and gardens of the farmers and were caught and tamed.

The advantage of having a herd of animals to furnish meat in lean seasons must have proved itself quickly. Later came the use of animals for milk giving and for riding, plowing, and burden bearing. These domesticated animals were a great aid to man's own strength.

Not all animals are useful or worth the trouble of taming. They must provide milk or meat or at least strength or speed for man, who otherwise would not be willing to share his food with them. They must be able to shift for themselves when they have grown past babyhood, and they themselves must be willing to exchange freedom for the comfort of a steady food supply. Some animals, such as the great solitary cats, never willingly trade the excitement of a hunting life for the dullness of captivity.

Some members of the wolf family had already become tamed while men were still hunters; the dog is by far man's oldest animal helper. Long before the dawn of history, however, most of our other animals had been tamed: cattle, hogs, sheep, camels, goats, donkeys, horses, as well as chickens and other birds of the Asiatic jungles.

Once settled down to farming and herd tending, people began to create a variety of useful things. Basketmaking was a very old craft, for baskets were useful in gathering food. When people began to live in villages, they learned to shape clay into pots and dishes and to bake them almost as hard as stone. At the same time they learned to spin thread by twisting together the long bast fibers which are to be found inside the stems of certain plants. After ages of spinning such fibers into fishing lines or knotting them into nets, and of weaving flexible plant stems into baskets and mats, someone put the two arts together and wove yarn into a wonderful new product, cloth. Meanwhile, men had learned to improve their ways of making stone weapons and tools. All of this made such a change in human life that we call it the Neolithic revolution, or, to put it more simply, the New Stone Age.

VILLAGERS BECOME TRADERS AND CITY DWELLERS. After a time, people saw that it was not necessary for everyone to do everything. Instead, the makers of pottery and clothing could trade their products to other people in return for food or other commodities. By 4000 B.C., little farming communities had sprung up thickly in the great river valleys of Asia and Africa. Now a second great change came about. This was the urban revolution, in which villages grew into cities. The making of textiles, pottery, metalwork, dyed and embroidered cloth, and jewelry became great industries, employing workers who could no longer produce their own food because they must spend all their time on their crafts.

From the cities, expeditions of traders went forth in search of raw materials. Rulers were eager for gold and precious stones, which they thought had the power of bringing health, long life, and prosperity. There were four great centers at this time. They were Egypt, Mesopotamia, India, and China. Trading parties met and began to draw ideas from one another. Exploring groups from these centers pushed even beyond the boundaries of the known world. Some of them may have reached the distant Americas.

By 3000 B.C., the early civilizations of the Old World had laid foundations of law, philosophy, religion, and art, and these were to become the basis of our own Western civilization. At this time, also, two bad practices developed from which man has not yet freed himself. Strong men made slaves of others, and conquest and war became a pattern of behavior.

NEOLITHIC REVOLUTION IN THE AMERICAS. While these things were going on in the rest of the world, what was happening to man in America? We look again at the New World with new eyes and new questions. From geology we learn that as the last ice-age glaciers began to melt away, conditions in North America changed very greatly. As ice sheets melted, areas of tundra or savanna favorable to herds and hunters changed. Then with the shifting patterns of wind and rain, hunting conditions became more difficult here also.

Knowing how the cities of the ancient world grew up along river valleys, we might hope to find early man settling down beside the Mississippi and the Amazon. But the great American rivers flowed within an area of heavy rainfull which produced forests unfavorable to large herds and thus to man. The Mississippi was not like the Nile, which overflowed at regular seasons, irrigating the wild grain, forcing the early Egyptians to drain swamps and to measure land again when property lines had washed away, and so to develop the mathematical science of geometry, or measurement of the earth. Nor were there, in North America, protected areas surrounded by deserts like the Nile valley. In America the nomadic hunters continued to pour down the Great Plains, falling upon the first farming settlements and raiding them.

Only in the Gila and lower Colorado river valleys of the Southwest were there settings somewhat like that of Egypt, where rivers ran through a warm, semidesert country. But there were no date palms or small grains here, and by the time the first farmers appeared, there were no horses or camels here to be tamed.

Then, too, the first people in these valleys had made a very long journey from the grim north. Perhaps the people who had lived through the effort of crossing the cold top of the world were not yet ready to develop a great civilization, similar to the civilizations of the Old World.

The English historian, Arnold J. Toynbee, says in this connection that sometimes, when a test is too severe, men manage to meet it by making a magnificent gesture, and then have no energy left for further progress. This, he says, is what happened to the Polynesians, who, in open canoes, crossed the vast Pacific to remote islands, but whose descendants forgot the skills necessary to make the long voyages that would liberate them from the island prisons on which they were born. Toynbee believes that the nomads who must wander as the climate changes are also "arrested" by the effort which this takes, and have no further energy left with which to develop the arts of civilization. Later we will see that this is what happened to the Indians of the Arctic.

Thus, the explanation of the failure of the Indians of North America to develop a civilization in the Gila and lower Colorado river valleys, where the setting was much like that of Egypt, may well be that the men who had so recently wandered across the Arctic path from Asia needed a time to rest in the sun, free from the pressure of new arrivals.

However this may be, the great changes that brought about the four great river civilizations of Egypt, India, China, and Mesopotamia failed to produce a similar result in the river valleys of North America. Folsom Man, after 10,000 B.C., left no more of his spear points in his old accustomed haunts. This may mean that the Folsom people moved away or died away, though we have no evidence that this is true. It may mean, indeed, that Folsom men no longer made their familiar weapons. Man is stubborn about giving up old ways of doing things, but now and then he does lose skills known to his ancestors, just as the descendants of the Polynesians lost the ability to cross the Pacific Ocean. On the ruins of many of the old civilizations of the ancient world live people who have forgotten the arts and languages of their ancestors. Yet the fact remains that caves which had once sheltered Folsom men showed subsequent earth deposits containing no trace of man; at least in such areas, some real event seems to have changed the story. In the following chapter we will see some of the evidences of time and change in our southwestern area.

IV. FOOD GATHERERS AND BASKETMAKERS

That Buffalo May Come

From far away frozen Buffalo Country
Hither now they come with their little ones,
Rapidly now they walk, rapidly they walk.
Even now they reach the Red Bird Gap.

Oh Buffalo Old Man! Oh Buffalo Old Woman!
Come hither rapidly with your little ones.
To Y'o pha k'ewe come with your little ones.

They bring to us long life together
And even now they reach Tesuque!

This song names the Great Plains and also a pass near the head of the Pecos River. Dr. Herbert Spinden translates "Y'o pha k'ewe," an old town of the Tesuque people, as "Cactus-row-ridge," which gives us a picture of the semidesert southwestern buffalo range.

The Indian title for this song is "Buffalo Magic Song, Making Come," and here are the last two lines, with Dr. Spinden's exact translation:

> *Ndin k'on wowatsi wogi*
>   They-to-us bring life together
> *Nä we ho'o in powa Te tsuge owinge.*
>   Here-at now they arrive Tesuque town-at.

FOOD GATHERERS AND BASKETMAKERS

OUR spotlight continues to focus upon the southwestern area,
not because no human activities were going on in the other
parts of the Americas but because the semidesert conditions of
the Southwest have preserved the story of the human settlements
that grew up after the nomadic hunting tribes had begun to settle
down here and there. Remember, as you read the following story,
that it was only one part of the vast drama that was taking place
all over the Americas.

Though the trail of Folsom Man seems to have ended in a
"Dead End Road" sign some ten thousand years B.C., we are left
with the question as to whether these hunters really disappeared
from the United States area or whether it was only that the Folsom
type of spear point fell into disuse.

Cochise Man. As we put the question of Folsom Man back on the shelf, let us examine some interesting artifacts discovered by school children playing in a gulch near Cochise, Arizona. These children found and brought to their teacher a number of strangely shaped stones. These were not spear points or hide scrapers but were flat stones hollowed out on one side. The teacher saw that they looked like the larger stones used by Indians for grinding corn. She knew that Stone Age men had used such stones for crushing seeds and nuts. Because the teacher knew how to ask the right questions of the right people, it was not long before anthropologists and geologists were happily at work studying the site where the children had found these stones.

After much work, the geologists were ready to give a rough date to the earth layers in which the stones were found. As they figured it, these tools had been used and lost not a few hundred years earlier, but something like fifteen thousand years ago! Though the scientists looked for spear points or other weapons at the Cochise site, they found nothing to show that these people had been hunters. Perhaps this had been a dry area with few game animals even at this early time, before the last Folsom spear point had fallen to earth.

Almost nothing else is known about the Cochise people; the curtain of mystery is pulled aside a minute and we see them there, gathering wild seeds and nuts and grinding them into a paste by means of stone grinders. Then the curtain comes down again, and we have no way of knowing what happened next. So far, the history of man in the Americas is like a peep show: "now you see him and now you don't."

The Cliff-dwelling Basketmakers. During all the thousands of years in which the Rocky Mountains and the Colorado plateau were rising, the rivers of the Southwest were working hard to stay at their old level, and in so doing they cut their way thousands of feet through layers of sandstone. Along the sides of these high cliffs which the rivers had cut, there were large natural ledges and caves which offered shelter and protection to man.

The hunters did not bury their dead in the caves they occupied. Perhaps they sent the sick or wounded or the old people away to die alone, as many primitive people have done. But somewhat before the time of Christ, some of the people of the Americas began to bury their dead and to put tools and weapons and personal possessions with their bodies, as the people of Egypt had done thousands of years earlier.

The semidesert dryness of the Southwest mummified the bodies in these graves and preserved the wooden and fiber objects buried with them. From these things we have learned a good deal about the people who lived in these caves before the time of Christ. They were very skillful weavers of baskets, so they are popularly called the Basketmakers. It is clear that they believed in a future life, for they buried treasures and foodstuffs with their dead. They even buried pet dogs, of breeds like our modern collies and spaniels, and they were thoughtful enough to bury red-painted deer bones with the bodies of their pets, so that the dogs might have food in the spirit world. Naturally, we want to know more about such people.

The Basketmakers used their baskets to gather wild rice, nuts, acorns, vegetables, fruits, and various seeds, some of which they stored away in storage pits dug in floors of caves. They may not have lived in the caves at all times, but they stored food and buried their dead in them and undoubtedly took refuge there in time of attack by their enemies.

From a study of the things they left behind them, we know that by their time the Southwest had already dried out into a semi-desert area. The vast bison herds which Sandia and Folsom men had hunted could no longer exist in such a country. There was only enough vegetation to support a limited number of animals, among which were deer, mountain sheep, rabbits, prairie dogs, and lesser creatures. The Basketmaker men hunted these animals by means of snares and nets. Some very large nets have been found in the grave pits. The spear, thrown by means of a spear thrower, was still used as a weapon, as it had been used in the Americas for some twenty thousand years. The time now came, however, when a new and important weapon appeared: the

bow and arrow, brought to America by new arrivals from Asia.

The finding of human remains of early American hunters is rare, but after the time of the Basketmakers there are plenty of bones and skulls to tell the anthropologists about the kind of people who came into the Americas. Anthropologists can tell a great deal about ancient men by the shapes of their skulls. You may have noticed that some people have heads that are almost round, whereas others have skulls that are narrower from side to side but longer from front to back. Scientists measure the skulls of ancient men very carefully to see if they are "roundheads" or "longheads," because this is one of the most important clues as to the part of the world from which a person's ancestors came.

The early Basketmakers were longheaded people. We even know how they arranged their hair. The men wore long loops at the sides of their faces and gathered the back hair into braids.

Women were content with a simple bob, perhaps because they needed human hair in making string, thongs, and basket handles, and could not persuade the men to give up their own hair.

Basketmaker clothes were simple loincloths for men and apron skirts for women. The interesting thing is that these garments were not made of skins but were actually of cloth, woven from fibers which women had chewed from the tough, swordlike leaves of the yucca plant. Both men and women wore square-toed sandals woven of plant fibers. Chiefs or other important people sometimes were buried in fur blankets. These had been made by cutting animal furs into strips and twisting the strips around stout yucca cords, which were then woven together.

A great variety of baskets have been found with the burials. Some were made of yucca fibers, others of shredded roots or of wooden splints. Many were decorated with designs that probably were magic spells to bring good luck. Some of the baskets were plastered inside with mud or piñon gum to make them watertight. Such baskets were used as cooking pots. Water was brought to a boil by dropping heated stones into the baskets.

As time went by, the people who lived in the cliff dwellings began to make pottery, which they decorated with a variety of colors and designs. Originally, man's use of pottery may have come about when some careless housewife left a clay-lined basket too close to the fire; this burned away the basket and baked the lining as hard as a stone. The Basketmakers, however, probably learned this art from more advanced people.

The first houses built by the Basketmakers were nothing more than enlarged copies of their storage pits, with shelters like lean-tos built above them. These pit houses were round or square, several feet deep, and lined with slabs of stone held up by posts. Roofs were made by means of slanting poles covered with brush and earth. Later houses were larger. Walls made of logs or poles chinked with mud grew higher, and roofs were made of timber instead of branches.

With the Cochise and the Basketmakers we have reached the food-gathering stage of human development. These people were no longer primarily hunters but had come to depend on vegetable foods for a good part of their diet. The Cochise may have caught small game with snares and nets. Perhaps they were like the Mojave Desert Indians of today, who have adapted themselves so well to their difficult country that they can find several dozen sources of food where a white man would starve.

People who meet such tests may survive yet have no energy left over for the production of the arts of civilization. The Cochise passed from the scene with nothing to their credit except that they had managed to feed themselves. The Basketmakers, with perhaps more adequate food, had energy left over for the weaving of baskets, sandals, coarse yucca textiles, and fur robes. Their burial customs show that their chieftains and priests had considerable power, which proves the existence of ritual and of political organization. The Basketmakers had begun to build simple houses and, in short, behaved like a settled agricultural people. They may have had vegetable plots which they tended. But theirs was an economy on a low scale of energy. With no domestic animals to furnish food and strength and no staple cereal as a food supply, they had no chance to develop a culture in which certain people would be freed from the job of food getting and thus could develop the crafts and arts.

Both peoples met the conditions of a hard country, the challenge of a drying-out land, and both were subject to pressure from the nomads who continued to appear from the north. To this pressure the Basketmakers made the successful response of hiding their settlements in ledges and caves in the cliffs. The evidence of the continued nomadic pressure lies in the appearance of the new weapon, the bow and arrow. For thousands of years the hunters in America had used spears and spear throwers, but how thoroughly the bow and arrow were accepted in America is shown by the fact that Indian arrowheads are a standard part of the trading equipment of small American boys in many parts of our country today.

Thus far, the Basketmakers had met the tests of life in a hard country and had resisted invasions from the north. Their real time of trouble lay ahead of them. The new danger was to come from a different and unexpected direction. To understand what it was, we must temporarily leave the Southwest and take a crow's flight southward for perhaps two thousand miles or so, to the place where the greatest event of pre-Columbian America may have taken place.

THE DISCOVERY OF MAIZE. The discovery of maize, or, as we more commonly know it, corn, was the great event of pre-Columbian America. Was corn developed slowly over hundreds of years from the seeds of a wild grass? Or did it spring more quickly from some wild ancestor, now lost, but perhaps like a small wild pod corn found in the highlands of Central America? However the cultivation of corn came about, this was the event from which the Indian civilizations grew. On the basis of this cereal supply, simple villages grew in time to be cities with great temples and palaces, as we will see in later chapters.

This event may have happened in middle America, perhaps in the highlands of Guatemala or Honduras. It may have come about in some such way as the imaginary story that follows.

It was a day in early autumn. A small group of women, dressed in brief aprons of animal skins, were leaving a sunny clearing on a hillside. Several brown and wiry children raced ahead of them, playing with thin, half-grown dogs. Blackened stumps over the whole of this wide hillside showed where the forest had been burned away—the lightning god had struck here. In the sunny clearing various small plants had sprung up. The women had found berries and plants with edible roots here in the spring, but the real treasure which had brought the tribe back to this region was the tall grass which bore large golden seeds in a husk. When green, these seeds were juicy and delicious, but, best of all, they dried to kernels which could be saved until times of scarcity when there were no other plant foods to be found and when the game resisted the magic spells and the spears of the hunters.

The children and dogs ran ahead of the women, who, having filled their baskets with the grain, were shelling some of it as they lingered in the pleasant sunshine of the clearing. Suddenly there was a great outcry from the children and an uproar from the dogs; the women saw a snarling, leaping flash of black and tawny yellow —the ocelot! Dropping their baskets, they ran to pull their children out of reach of the whirling cyclone of claws and teeth where the ocelot and the dogs fought—but one of the boys lay still, his throat and face torn by the maddened animal. The ocelot escaped, followed by the yelping dogs.

Beside the dead boy, mingled with his blood in the dust, were the scattered grains, trampled into the ground; the women would not return to this place again. But the following year was a bad time. There was a long drought: game was scarce. Men returned from the hunt empty-handed, and women found only a few roots and grains to carry back to camp. The time came when hunger drove the women back to the clearing where the ocelot had killed the boy. As they approached they glanced about with fear, as if the place were haunted by the boy who had been slain. But when they reached the place where the struggle had taken place they forgot their fears; on the very spot where the boy had been killed, there was a large patch of the food-bearing grain. As the women gathered it, they talked again about the thing that had happened; it was as if their lost grain had come to life in the form of new plants. How wonderful it would be if they always had such a harvest! The wiser ones among them wondered and pondered; they remembered all that they had noticed about the grain, how kernels left in damp places had sprouted, how patches of the grass sprang up where lightning had burned the forest away.

How many times had events like this happened, and in how many places, before the hunters discovered that by planting the grain and tending the patches of plants that grew, they could be sure of a food supply? Somehow they learned to burn the forest, to put the seed in the ground; as they did so, they spoke and sang and danced the magic rites and made sacrifices to the gods of sun and rain and earth.

ABOUT TIME SCALES. In the discussions of Sandia and Folsom men we measured time in thousands of years, using the science of geology to date the earth layers in which the stone tools and broken bones were found. But when people began to settle down beside corn patches, to make pottery and to build shelters, they quite unknowingly furnished anthropologists with ways of dating the story of man's past much more accurately. You may wonder how a broken bit of pottery or the half-burned beam of an ancient house could possibly show an archaeologist how long ago it had been made and used.

As the scientists dug into trash heaps or the ruins of ancient dwelling sites, they found that if these sites had lain undisturbed during the centuries since men had lived there, the objects found in them occurred in a certain order. That is, there were certain styles of crude pottery which were buried most deeply, whereas other styles were found near the top of the ground. Usually the top layers contained objects that were more artistic and elaborate, and sometimes it might be seen that some of the designs had been borrowed from other people living elsewhere. Obviously the things at the bottom had been used and thrown away much earlier, to be covered by the dust and the castoff objects of later centuries. By studying the layers of earth above these, geologists were able to estimate how long ago they had lain on the surface of the ground. Today, objects from the most widely scattered rubbish heaps can be dated by what is called "cross reference"—that is, we know their age because they are like others the ages of which have been learned from the undisturbed layers of earth. The shape, the clay, and the decoration of a pottery object tell the anthropologists when and where it was made.

THE TREE-RING CALENDAR. An astronomer gave archaeologists another way of dating Indian ruins. Dr. A. E. Douglas, director of the astronomical observatory of the University of Arizona, noticed that the growth rings of trees were thick in wet years and thin in dry ones. Furthermore, he saw that the wet and dry years matched the cycle of sun storms that make dark spots on the sun. It is known that every eleven years a certain cycle of storm comes, another occurs every fifty-five years, and a still longer one every two hundred and twenty-two years. These patterns can be figured back thousands of years into the past.

Dr. Douglas saw that tree trunks of the dry Southwest always faithfully record the conditions during the growth season. It occurred to him that if trees are such good year keepers, then the posts and beams found in ancient Indian dwellings could be used to date the ruins, by comparing their growth rings with the records of sunspot cycles.

Dr. Douglas began a study of beams taken from old Indian dwellings. Each time he found an older beam whose growth rings fitted into his series, he pushed his tree calendar a few years farther into the past. Since burnt wood, if it has not crumbled, shows the growth rings, Dr. Douglas could date even the ruins of dwellings destroyed by fire long ago.

At last his tree-ring calendar reached back to the time of Christ. Within this period of almost two thousand years, any ancient beam in the arid Southwest can be dated. If growth rings show that the tree was cut in 599 A.D., then the dwelling in which the beam was used must have been built shortly after this date. Once this is known, the scientists can give a date to the pottery or stone objects found among the ruins, which makes it possible for us to date accurately the two-thousand-year story of the Pueblo people whom we shall meet in the following chapter.

V. CITADELS
OF THE SOUTHWEST

Song of the Sky Loom

Oh our Mother the Earth, oh our Father the Sky,
Your children are we, and with tired backs
We bring you the gifts that you love.
Then weave for us a garment of brightness;
May the warp be the white light of morning,
May the weft be the red light of evening,
May the fringes be the falling rain,
May the border be the standing rainbow.
Thus weave for us a garment of brightness
That we may walk fittingly where birds sing,
That we may walk fittingly where grass is green,
Oh our Mother the Earth, oh our Father the Sky!

In the semidesert Southwest a distant rain looks like the hanging
looms upon which Indians weave blankets. This poem is an Indian way
of praying, "Give us this day our daily bread." It asks that men may
walk fittingly in a good world where birds sing and grass is green. We
later Americans, living in an age in which forests and grasslands have
been almost destroyed and precious topsoil allowed to erode, could
profit much from adopting the Indian feeling for "our Mother the
Earth."

CITADELS OF THE SOUTHWEST

Invasion from Mexico? In the southwestern part of the United States area, the semidesert earth has preserved a long story of man's passing. Here, as we saw, bands of hunters lived ten and twenty thousand years ago. Here seed gatherers ground wild seeds on their stone grinders. Here Basketmakers lived in cliff and mesa communities. Some of these became ghost towns long ago, and the dust of years covered the objects which anthropologists have dug up and studied. Later towns, such as a Hopi pueblo called Oraibi, in Arizona, have been lived in for a thousand or more years. By comparison with them, the Virginia town of Jamestown, established in 1607 and sometimes called the earliest American settlement, was built only yesterday. Yet even these old pueblos were young in comparison with Indian settlements farther south in Mexico and Central America. In later chapters you will read about these cities; in this one you need to know that they did exist and that in some way a wave of people, or perhaps only of trade objects and ideas, came northward to change the lives of the people who lived in the cliffs and on the mesas.

The development of a corn culture was without doubt the big event that made possible the growth of the Southwestern Indian communities which the Spaniards later called "pueblos," from their word for "town." Several centuries later, beans also were brought northward. With this new food supply, the people of the Southwest had the energy to develop arts and crafts and religious rituals. Some wanderers from the south may also have brought the skills of silver working, the practice of head flattening, cremation of the dead, the worship of the turkey, and details of art, architecture, and religious ritual. The Indians of the Southwest raised different varieties of corn from those of the Mexicans and Mayas, and they had different gods and religious beliefs. The clues point only to a slow seeping of ideas into North America from Mexico.

THE PUEBLO COMMUNITIES. Pueblo, as we have seen, was the Spanish term for the communal dwellings white men found in the Southwest, a name still used for these towns and for the Indians who live in them. Many readers of this book come from families that have been in America for over three hundred years. But young Pueblo people who read it may have had ancestors in America for ten thousand years; their ancestry may go back to the cliff dwellers. Many of the pueblos were built in ledges or against cliffs, others in valleys. Some were on the mesas or "tables" of

rock that towered above the plateau. One pueblo in New Mexico, called Acoma, was built on a mesa three hundred and fifty-seven feet above the plain. Timbers were cut in forests twenty miles away and were dragged up the narrow footpath to the top of the mesa to build Acoma. There are ancient Indian legends of an even older town on the nearby Mesa Encantata, or "Enchanted Mesa," left uninhabited when an earthquake destroyed the footpath leading to it one day when the village people were working in their fields on the plain below.

You can probably imagine why people went to so much hard work to build their homes on the tops of mesas high above their fields. The farmers who grew corn in the valleys and who made pottery and cloth and other things in their pueblos were the envy of wandering hunters who continued to pour down from the north. The Pueblo Indians built their homes in cliffs and on mesas in order to be able to protect them. With springs to furnish water, and dried corn and beans for food, they could sit behind their walls and defend themselves by arrows and spears until the invaders grew tired and went away.

Pueblo Daily Life. The raising of corn on the arid southwestern plains was quite another thing from raising corn in the fertile, wet plateaus of Mexico or the jungles of Yucatán. The Pueblos developed a variety of corn with long, deep-growing roots well suited to a dry country. Even so, they had to irrigate their sun-parched fields. In the valley of the Salt River, which runs into the Gila in Arizona, ancient peoples cultivated perhaps a quarter

of a million acres. Drainage ditches have been uncovered that were seven feet deep and thirty feet wide. In some places canals stretched for twenty-five miles.

In the pueblos each member of the family had his own tasks. Men and boys hunted, quarried, tended the irrigation ditches, and did the heavier work in the fields. Women and girls usually did the spinning, weaving, and pottery making, though in some towns men were the weavers and potters. Young girls helped grind the corn, using stone rolling pins and grinding stones called "metates." The coarse meal made on rough metates was ground finer on smoother ones. Then the little brown hands of girls and women slapped the batter of dampened meal into thin cakes, and the cakes were baked on flat stones in open fireplaces.

Throughout many ages, such little hands slapped adobe plaster on the insides of pueblos, leaving prints we can see today. When skins and blankets were thrown over benches, placed against the walls, housekeeping could begin. Water was brought to the pueblo in jars carried on the head. Corn and beans and squash were tended, gathered, and cooked. Blankets, cloth, baskets, and pottery were made.

By 800 A.D. the Pueblos had learned to weave cloth of various types. They had no sheep to furnish wool. The Basketmakers had discovered how to weave the fibers of the native yucca plant, and the early Pueblos cultivated and spun cotton, a plant which may have come to them from farther south. They also made embroidery. Masks and costumes of dancers and others who took part in religious ceremonies were decorated with skins and featherwork.

Styles in baskets and pottery changed slowly as time went on. The drawing of designs on beautifully shaped pottery jars and bowls became an art. Ancient Pueblo potters probably worked almost exactly as modern ones do. Today the work is usually done by a woman who sits on the ground with her materials around her. The jars, shaped of clay and sun-dried, are painted. The brushes used for the painting of designs are slender sections of yucca leaf, one end of which has been chewed to remove the pulp and free the fine fibers. Dipping her brush in colors made by grinding iron oxide and other minerals or plants in water, the artist draws her design on the dish or bowl and paints in the details. Then the jars are fired in a big outdoor stove, called a kiln, to harden the clay.

RITES AND FESTIVALS. All was not work. Every season was celebrated with ritual ceremonies. The dances and prayers were meant to bring rain, good luck in hunting, and protection from enemies, but this was only half the matter. The Indians saw themselves as a necessary part in a great drama of creation that went on continually between man and nature. Man's part was to worship the gods with praise and sacrifices. In return, the gods of the earth and sky would give man the food and drink that he needed. Mother Earth would give him plants and animals, with the help of rain and sun from Father Sky. The "plumed serpent," which was both bird and snake, was the symbol of the union between the two, or of life itself, of breath, of motion. The figure of the plumed serpent appeared in the textiles, pottery, and ornaments of the people of the Southwest and on the walls of the kivas, or sacred underground chambers used for religious ceremonies. The winged serpent design was used to an even greater extent in Mexico and Yucatán.

Dramatic dances were anything but light social affairs. Handed down from father to son for hundreds of years, they were the serious and sacred business of life. In the dance rituals the Indians acted out their idea of the relationship between man and the gods. These beautiful dances also celebrated the various seasons. The Sun Dance, for example, was a prayer of thanksgiving for the return of the sun, which brought the new growing season after the winter. The series of Corn Dances were prayers for the successful growing of the crop and also of thanksgiving for the harvest. The Eagle Dance praised the sky powers and asked

their help. The Buffalo Dance was a symbol of the relationship
between the hunters and the animals they hoped to kill for the
winter's food. Taken together, the rites throughout the four seasons of the year traced the pattern of man's dependence upon
nature.

The children of the Pueblos had to learn the chants and the
dances and arts and crafts in order to carry on the life of the tribe.
Of course, this was exactly what they wanted to do. Wild horses
could not have dragged them away from the dances and ceremonies that they were allowed to see and to join. As for the mysterious religious rites that went on in the kivas, boys could scarcely
wait to grow up and to be allowed to take part in them.

Meanwhile, mothers and grandmothers and old men told the
children tales about men and animals and gods. The Pueblos were
great storytellers and had no competition from funny papers,
comic books, radio, and movies. Pueblo children learned the
dances, rites, arts, and stories that their ancestors had known for
hundreds of years before them. Children were made to feel that
they were necessary and important. As they grew up, they did
not want to break away from the group or from the old ways. So
there was little change as each generation came and went.

It is likely that the ancient communities were governed like
those of today. The Pueblos did not band together to form a state
or a nation. Instead, each small pueblo was separate and independent, ruled by its own council of elder leaders. The chief active
officers were elected. There may have been civil rulers, like the
present governors, and military rulers, like the war captains who
now concern themselves chiefly with policing the boundaries, the
stock, and the festivals.

There was no such thing as private ownership of land. The
earth belonged to everyone. Each farmer used what the leaders
felt he needed and would care for. People worked together at
building and tending the irrigation ditches and the places of

worship. They helped one another in the building of new rooms for growing families. It was a good system and one which suited the Pueblos. This was, in fact, the Indian way over most of the Americas, and it was generally successful.

As time passed, the pueblos became larger, but they never became real cities, perhaps because there was never enough food for a large population. More and more rooms were added at the sides of the pueblos or built on the tops as extra stories. You may some day visit Pueblo Bonito, or "Beautiful Town," which is the largest of the twelve pueblos in Chaco Canyon, New Mexico. This pueblo was started about 500 A.D. and was inhabited until at least 1100 A.D. After that, its owners seem to have walked off and left it.

Pueblo Bonito is a large, four-story apartment house built in a semicircle around a central plaza, which was used as a stage for dances and rites. The oldest parts of Pueblo Bonito were built of rough sandstone slabs. From century to century other rooms were added, until at last there were eight hundred of them. Some fifteen hundred people may have lived there. The newest walls were of hand-dressed stone placed in neat layers.

Pueblo Bonito and the other large pueblos were in some ways like the cooperative apartment houses of today which are owned by a number of families. The Indian families, which are called "clans," kept the same rooms in these community houses until the clan died out. This happened not only when there were many deaths in the family but also when too many sons were born. When a man married he moved into his wife's clan, building a new room there if necessary. Thus a family that had a great many daughters suddenly became much larger. But if only sons were born, then when these married and moved away the clan disappeared.

THE GREAT BUILDING TIME. The pueblos were part of a great wave of building which followed the change from a hunting life to that of corn and bean culture. A thousand years after Christ, the Indians of the Americas were building temples by the scores everywhere from the Mississippi valley to Peru. Thousands of small mounds topped by altars were going up along the Mississippi and Ohio rivers. In the Southwest, tons of stone and timber and mortar were used to build the apartment dwellings and the underground temples or kivas. In Mexico the Toltecs were piling up enormous pyramids, on the tops of which temples were built. In Central America the Mayas were also building great pyramids, upon which they constructed strikingly beautiful buildings. And down in South America, high in the Andes, the pre-Incaic peoples were carrying on remarkable engineering feats. Over in Europe a fever of religious feeling was also beginning to express itself in the magnificent cathedrals of the Middle Ages. This was also the period of the Viking voyages of discovery, and it was just before the era called the Renaissance, when all of Europe was afire with a new enthusiasm for learning and for creation.

Do you think that some change in the weather may have had something to do with all this activity? Could it have been true that for a period of several hundred years it was neither too hot nor too cold nor too wet, but just wet and sunny enough for good crops and cool enough to make people feel full of energy and enthusiasm?

HARD TIMES COME TO THE PUEBLOS. The Pueblos remained a small-town people, unlike the city-building Indians of Mexico, Yucatán, and South America. Even in their most flourishing period they did not carve gigantic idols or build great pyramids and temples. Instead, they were content to make small art objects: carved bracelets and rings, turquoise and silver ornaments, painted jars and bowls, woven and embroidered textiles. They became skilled craftsmen but not great builders and artists. Even at best, it was not easy to make a living on their arid plateaus. Farming required much time and work in hauling water and tending the

PUEBLO ART
Left, elkskin mask, Zuni Pueblo; center, Pueblo pottery water jars; right, dance mask, Zuni Pueblo

irrigation ditches. Crops were not as abundant as they were in warm, damp regions farther south. With an excess of food, man has time for other things, but the Pueblos more or less broke even. A time came when they could not do even that.

Pueblo Bonito, in Chaco Canyon, was abandoned some time in the twelfth century. By the time Columbus discovered America, many other pueblos were falling into ruins. Chaco Canyon today has no river within a radius of more than fifty miles. Yet ruins of fields, irrigation ditches, and villages tell us that many thousands of people once lived there.

There is no doubt that in early Pueblo days water flowed in the many other canyons where ruins are found. This land continued to become dryer and dryer, as it had been doing for hundreds of years. Juicy grass and plants were replaced by tough, semidesert plants. To make matters worse, the growth rings of trees show that there was a severe drought between 1275 and 1310 A.D., which must have caused many streams and springs to dry up. The great herds that roamed this country in the time of Folsom

Man had disappeared long before this. Now even the deer and rabbits and smaller animals must have almost died away as springs dried up.

When the drought killed their crops, the people must have felt that their gods were angry and had turned against them. Of course, they could not know that it was not their fault that the land was drying up. It is likely that they made desperate efforts to satisfy the angry gods. At first, the elders of the tribes may have planned new building programs to occupy idle hands and to try to please the gods. In some of these ancient towns there are as many as fifty of the sacred kivas.

By the end of the great building period, the Pueblos were already living in a smaller area than the Basketmakers had occupied. During the long drought of the thirteenth century, as water sources dried away and people could no longer irrigate their crops, the communities began to break up. The time came when, in order to find drinking water, people had to go away from the places where their ancestors had lived for hundreds of years. Many must have died of hunger and thirst. As the survivors gathered around the few remaining springs and rivers, probably there was trouble among the various tribes.

Those who managed to survive became extremely conservative. As their outside world shrank, they turned more desperately to religion, in the hope that the ancient rites might help them regain the "good old days" of their ancestors. Thus they preserved long and exact rituals of song and dance, fasting, prayer, and sacrifice.

Coronado and his Spanish conquistadors arrived in 1540 in search of the seven golden cities described by Cabeza de Vaca. However, they found only what they contemptuously called "poor mud villages," so they left this area alone. In later days, our own land-grabbing American ancestors were happy to bypass this land of sand and scrub, rattlesnake, and broiling sun, which they, too, did not consider worth taking away from the Indians. The Hopi

were living in seven pueblos when the Spaniards arrived, and
today they are still living in six of them.

Hard times had forced the Pueblo Indians into such an intense
inner life that even our early Indian Administration, which tried
in every way to break up the old Indian patterns of living, was
unable to force them to relinquish the old ways. Today there are
sixteen thousand people in the pueblos. They still use secret rites
that are hundreds of years old; they guard these rites carefully, as
a most precious heritage.

How America's Most Ancient Art Gallery Was Discovered.
Unfortunately, some of the most interesting art of the Pueblo
people disappeared when the plastered adobe walls of underground kivas crumbled into dust. Yet thanks to archaeology, some
of this art may be seen today. In New Mexico there is what might
be called the oldest "art gallery" in the United States. This is how
it was discovered.

Archaeologists knew that in 1598, twenty-two years before the
Pilgrims landed on Plymouth Rock, a Spanish governor had led an
expedition north from Mexico into what is now New Mexico and
that one of his followers had written this account of what he saw:

> The Indians took the priests to the quarters which had been pre-
> pared for them. The walls of their rooms were cleanly swept. The next
> day, however, when the whitewash had dried, we were able clearly to
> see through the whitewash, paintings which made our blood run cold.
> . . . On the walls of the room where we were quartered were many
> paintings of the demons they worship as gods. Fierce and terrible were
> their features. It was easy to understand the meaning of these for the
> god of water was near the water, the god of the mountains was near
> the mountains, and in like manner all those deities they adore, their
> gods of the hunt, crops, and other things they have.

Though Spanish blood had run cold at the sight of these paintings, the very thought of such pictures made the archaeologists'
blood run hot. They searched ruined Pueblo mounds along the

banks of the Rio Grande, hoping to find a clue. At last, in one mound eroded by rain, searchers found a fragment of a sword forged in Spain and bits of porcelain never made by Indian hands. Two miles away, other Spanish objects were found amid what was left of ancient plazas, houses, and burial grounds. Legend called these ancient settlements Puaray and Kuaua.

Archaeologists sliced through the mounds, cleaned the ancient plazas, and dug into the underground kivas. They unearthed a thousand skeletons and quantities of pottery and other Indian objects.

One hot summer day four years later, as they were excavating one of the kivas, they came upon the trail of the lost murals. They had found many of these kivas, most of which were ten to twelve feet below the surface, round or square in shape, and from fifteen to thirty feet in diameter. The Spaniards had called them *estufas*, or ovens. On this hot afternoon, workers were digging crumbled adobe out of a large, square kiva on a plaza of the village. A fragment caught the attention of Gordon Vivian, supervisor of the excavation. He saw that a streak of color ran across this part of the ancient clay wall. With a shout he stopped the work and called the other archaeologists. The lump of adobe was tested with a pocketknife. It split evenly along the line of the band of color. On the inner surface, workers saw an unmistakable drawing of two fingers of a human hand.

Full of excitement, they scrambled into the pit to examine what was left of its inner walls. They found a treasure trove. Eighty-five successive plasterings had been put on the wall, and at least seventeen of them showed remnants of ancient pictures. Almost half of the wall was still standing.

The archaeologists looked at it with despair. What science could strip those paper-thin layers of plaster from that wall without causing it to crumble into dust? It was clear that the wall must be moved to the shelter of the University of New Mexico laboratory before its secrets could safely be wrested from it. But how to move an ancient wall even eighteen miles? The wall weighed many tons and would fall apart at any careless slip.

Nevertheless, the job was done. First the adobe walls were blanketed with many layers of soft tissue paper. Each wall was wrapped in burlap soaked in plaster of Paris. Then a wooden framework was fastened around it, followed by more layers of plaster-soaked burlap reinforced with steel rods. The wall was now ready for its dangerous journey.

The journey was made, the wall was set up again in the big laboratory. When the plaster jackets were removed, the workers had the delicate job of stripping off each one of the eighty-five ancient plaster layers. First the plaster surface was coated with collodion, and sheets of soft muslin were pressed against it. Later the muslin was carefully pulled away, bringing with it the most recent plaster layer which ancient Indian hands had patted on the wall. Human eyes could again look on what had made Spanish blood run cold almost three and a half centuries earlier.

The first picture the workers found was that of a horizontal human figure with a fantastic headdress—obviously a representation of death. Following another such layer there appeared an elaborately costumed dancer. As layer after layer of this amazing picture book was stripped from the kiva wall, other strange figures came to view. There were dancers in bizarre masks. There were animals, birds, corn and other plants, altars with rain clouds above them, and symbols of rain, lightning, and thunder.

As picture after picture was revealed, each was photographed. Then each layer was pulled away from the wall and glued firmly to wallboard. They may be seen today in the museum at Santa Fe, their brilliant colors unfaded after almost four centuries. The kiva wall was moved back to its old site, to become part of the state-owned Coronado Monument.

THE PEOPLE OF THE GALLINA TOWERS. At about the time that

Pueblo Bonito was abandoned, a century or so before Columbus was born, a group of people who had built tall stone towers in wooded canyons of New Mexico came to an even more sudden and violent end.

Along the Gallina and other river canyons of New Mexico there are hundreds of towers built of roughly squared sandstone blocks put together with adobe mortar. Ladders gave access to holes in the roofs, by which the owners entered. Inside the towers, ladders led down into rooms with smoothly plastered walls, on which were paintings of birds and plants. Benches against the walls served as seats and as storage spaces for colored face powder, ornaments cut from shells, clothing made of skins and feathers, feathered prayer sticks, arrows, weapons, and tools.

In one tower archaeologists discovered the bones of the Gallina people themselves. Sixteen skeletons of men and women were found, together with the bows and arrows with which the people were defending themselves when burning wooden timbers of the roof crashed down on their heads. Further study made it clear that before each tower was burned, it had been defended to the last by men and women warriors.

By studying growth rings on beams in the towers, archaeologists learned that the trees with which the towers were built had been cut between 1143 and 1248 A.D. A study of the skeletons, the pottery, and the utensils of the people showed that they were not Pueblos. They may have moved to New Mexico from another region.

Who killed them? The evidence lies in the arrowheads found in the bodies. They were small and triangular flints like those made by the Pueblos.

Such has been the long story of the Basketmaker Pueblos. It has been a long story because Pueblo history is better known than that of many other tribes. Even in the Southwest there were other groups living elsewhere in the mountains and the semidesert regions. Many of these other people had been there as long as the Basketmaker Pueblos of the plateau region. Still other Indian groups were almost newcomers to the Southwest. The Navaho and Apache tribes had been there only a century or so when Columbus discovered America. The Apaches never really settled down even in all this time. They remained hunters and raiders, like other nomadic peoples from the north who had harassed the Pueblos from time to time during their long history.

VI. INTERLUDE: THE VIKINGS FIND AND LOSE AMERICA

Thorhall's Song on Leaving America

I was told when I came here
That I should have the best of drink.
This country seems to me most drear;
Plain water from the well-spring's brink,
O'er which I stoop to fill my pail
(A warrior trained to fight in mail),
Is all the wine I've ever tasted,
My sojourn here is surely wasted.

Viking adventurers named an icy island "Greenland" and our cold northern coast "Vinland." In this poem Thorhall expresses his indignation at having been misled by Leif Ericson's glowing accounts of Vinland and decides that his stay there has been wasted.

INTERLUDE: THE VIKINGS
FIND AND LOSE AMERICA

I**T WAS** a cold day in the late summer of 986 A.D., and a bluster-
ing wind from the north lashed the Atlantic Ocean into great
waves. The storm had been raging for days. The men in the
battered little boat with the dragon carved on the prow were dead
tired and half starved; they wished with all their hearts that they
had never left their comfortable homes in Iceland to set sail for
Greenland. Even Bjarni Herjolsson, to whom the dragon ship
belonged, had to admit that the lashing winds had blown them
off their course. They should long before have reached Greenland,
where he was going to join his father, who had followed Eric the
Red when this quick-tempered adventurer had had to leave
Iceland.

At last they saw land ahead, but their hearts sank when they reached it. The shore stretched empty before them: no masts of ships, no feast-hall roofs. They were hungry for their own kind, for feasts and meetings with friends and relatives, for food and wine and songs, and for the sagas, or stories of Viking heroes which the music-making *skalds* sang to the sound of the harp. None of these things was here. When the winds died down, they turned back north again and after many days reached Greenland.

During the long winter evenings in Greenland, Bjarni often told of the unknown land that he had discovered. Among the people who asked him eager questions about it was young Leif, one of Eric's sons. As he listened, Leif's mind began to burn with the desire to explore this unknown country. Years later he bought a boat from Bjarni, fitted it with provisions, and persuaded thirty-five of his friends to set off on the adventure with him. He even induced old Eric the Red to lead the expedition, in order to bring it luck. Eric protested that he was too old to go, but Leif outtalked him. At last the day came when they rode down to the shore to set sail. But Eric's horse stumbled, and the old explorer fell and hurt his foot. Eric took this as a bad sign. "I am not destined to discover more countries than this in which we are now living," he told his son. "We shall no longer keep one another company."

Leif sadly said good-by to his father and turned the dragon prow of his ship toward the land which Bjarni had sighted. They found the new land and went ashore, but it was a poor, cold place of glaciers and flat rock. Leif said, "Unlike Bjarni, we have not failed to come ashore in this country, and I shall now give it a name and call it 'Helluland' (land of flat stones)." Then the party pushed on to discover a new coast with long white beaches backed by woods. Here Leif said, "This land shall be given a name after its nature and shall be called 'Markland' (woodland)."

Then Leif turned his ship to the open sea and sailed with a northeast wind for two days. Again land was sighted.

And such land! Rich, grassy meadows for the cattle, tall trees that would make wonderful ships' masts, waters that swarmed with fish. Scholars now think that this land, which Leif called "Vinland," was the coast of North America somewhere south of the Saint Lawrence River.

Leif divided his party into two groups; each day one group went exploring while the other group rested and took care of the camp. Leif ordered his men to stick together, since it would be a serious thing to be lost in this vast country. But one night the exploring party came home without Thyrker, whom Leif had loved almost as his own father since childhood. Furious and frightened, Leif started out with a searching party of twelve men. After a while they came across Thyrker, who told them in great excitement that he had discovered wild grapes. Now they could make wine! Calling his men together the next day, Leif told them, "We will now do two things. Each day we will either gather grapes or we will fell trees for a cargo for my ship."

When the ship was loaded with wild grapes and timber, they set sail back to Greenland. His adventures earned him a new name—Leif the Lucky.

The year was 1003 A.D. Leif Ericson had brought the white man's cross and sword to the American continent—a thousand years after the time of Christ and very nearly a thousand years ago.

Other sons of Eric the Red made less lucky voyages; one was buried in America. A daughter, Freydis, half sister of Leif, led one of the five later voyages which are described in the sagas. When her companions did not please Freydis, she murdered several of them, women and children, with an ax. Other women came here; the sagas name a baby, Snorri, the first known white child born in the Americas. The histories of these expeditions were told and retold by the *skalds* who sang the sagas in the feast halls of Iceland. Three hundred years afterward, the sagas were first written down.

You may wonder how much to believe of stories that were first told three centuries before they were written down. But a careful check with historic records proves that the Icelandic sagas were very true accounts, and so we may believe that those sagas dealing with "Wineland the Good" or, as they called it, Vinland, are actual reports carried home by America's earliest known white explorers. Two Scandinavian historians, writing in 1076 and in 1140, mention the Norse discovery of Vinland, the new land beyond Thule, which may have been Iceland or the Faroe Islands. They appear to consider the discovery a fact well known to everyone.

The sagas are not the only clues to this story of the Viking explorations in the Americas. In Nova Scotia and elsewhere in the northeastern part of the United States, Viking axes, boat keels, and other objects have been found, including curiously marked stones which puzzle scholars. Olaf Strandwold has written a study called *Norse Inscriptions on American Stones,* telling about more than thirty of these stones. Some of them, he says, are road markers set up to show later explorers which way a certain party had gone. Others were put up to mark the site of religious celebrations. He reads one stone found in Braxton County, West Virginia, as an account of a colony of Norsemen who settled there; among them were people named Qn Eric, Rikar, Ole, and a woman called Guri. He dates this stone about 1037, believing that had it been later, certain Danish letter types would have been used. A second clue to the date lies in the fact that the forms of the cross and of the letter A used on this stone were given up after the first half of the eleventh century. A New England stone bearing such a cross carries a date which in our calendar would be 1031 A.D.

This Qn Eric, writes Professor Strandwold, was quite a wanderer. At one time this Viking selected the Great Mound (described on page 128) as the site of a Yule festival. Arriving back at his main settlement in Massachusetts, he carved on a stone:

"Overland Route—Qn set the marker." A stone found in New England, says Professor Strandwold, tells that Qn Eric met his death when a boat turned over, and concludes with the words: "The ice owns Qn. O Tiv, raise him to everlasting light."

Many more Norsemen than are mentioned in the Icelandic sagas must have come to America. It may be that adventurers from Norway, unknown to the *skalds* who retold the Icelandic stories, set up other colonies far inland.

The Annals kept yearly in Iceland during the discovery period mention several visitors to the new land. In 1121 the Annals note the departure of "Eric, Bishop of Greenland," for Vinland. Nothing more is heard of Bishop Eric—unless, of course, he should be that Qn Eric who left so many marker stones in America. In 1347 the Icelandic Annals note that "A ship which had sailed to Markland came to Iceland with eighteen men on board." This note in the Icelandic Annals closes the book on the American adventure.

After that, bad days came to the Viking colonists. For several hundred years the Vikings had sailed up the rivers in almost every part of Europe, leaving tall, blond rulers even in remote Russia. Now Iceland, which had been settled since 874 A.D., was no longer a prosperous settlement sending out its adventurous sons. At home in Norway there were wars and rebellions. The little colonies in Greenland, and possibly in America, whose settlers had looked forward each summer to a ship or two from the homeland, bringing news and food and wine, were neglected. Years passed; after 1347 no more ships went to Markland or Vinland. The settlements died away. Their very names were forgotten.

The saga spotlight fell upon the few individuals who returned successfully home to Iceland with their cargoes of wood and wine and their stories of Vinland the Good. But what of other colonists who may have remained in the new land? What did they think when no more ships came from home? What did they do? If Viking parties really wandered inland far enough to use the Great Mound for Yule ceremonies, their explorations were more extensive than any reported in the sagas. But America's vast spaces may have been too much for them, and their numbers too few, so that in the end they were swallowed up by the forests. The first invasion of America by the white man rippled out into silence.

VII. THE MOUND BUILDERS

Iroquois Dirge

Woe! Woe!
Hearken ye!
We are diminished!
Woe! Woe!
The cleared land has become a thicket.
Woe! Woe!
The clear places are deserted.
Woe!
They are in their graves—
They who established it—
Woe!
The great League.
Yet they declared
It should endure—
The great League.
Woe!
Their work has grown old.
Woe!
Thus we are become miserable.

White settlers were surprised at the oratorical and political skill of the Iroquois who lived in the eastern forests. This Iroquois dirge laments the passing of the great League, a tribal organization which may have been patterned on a much earlier Mound Builder confederacy. It may serve as a dirge for the lost culture of the Mound Builders and for forgotten rituals once held before the temple mounds which dotted the central part of our country before and after the Vikings discovered it.

THE MOUND BUILDERS

SEVERAL centuries before the Viking exploration of our northeastern coasts in the eleventh century A.D., there may have
been another and more successful invasion and colonization of the
central portion of our country. We do not know definitely that this
is what happened, but let us consider the evidence that such an
event took place, only to be more thoroughly forgotten than was
the Viking invasion of a later century.

When you consider that this possible event must have happened
well over a thousand years ago, in a part of our country where
damp forests and the ravages of flood waters quickly destroy all

objects not made of stone, you can understand that such invaders could have appeared and disappeared, leaving no trace.

If the Norsemen had been settlers with a talent for friendship instead of plunderers with a habit of fighting, they might have left us a saga describing the Mound Builders of the Mississippi and the Ohio river systems, whose fascinating culture must have been in full flower at about the time of the Viking discovery of America. Since we have no such saga, we must fall back on our own imagination to visualize the life that lay behind the artifacts which anthropologists have dug from the mounds left by these people.

Let us imagine that our Eric, Bishop of Greenland, who set sail for Vinland, never to be heard from again, was one of those left behind in America by some Viking ship that met disaster and failed to return. Surviving his comrades, Eric at length left his settlement and wandered westward, where he was captured by a trading party from a Mound Builder center. Unlike the men of Leif's settlement, Eric was a crusading Christian who felt that it was his mission to bring the cross to these children of God. His courage and kindliness so impressed his captors that in time he was given his freedom. Our imaginary scene takes place some time later in an important Mound Builder settlement. The time is around 1036 A.D., and the village is in a state of great activity because this is the day following the death of a great chief who had been the head of a confederacy of Indian tribes that were scattered over the central plains.

MAIN STREET IN MOUNDSVILLE. Eric the Viking, who had lived for some years in America, was taking a walk through the village of the tribe that had adopted him. Most of the other able-bodied men of the village were hard at work digging and carrying earth for the new burial mound on the outskirts of the town. Stakes had been driven in the ground to trace the outlines of the new mound, so that workers would know where to dump their baskets of earth. Eric had been lending a hand as they burned and scraped the timbers to line the grave and constructed the shrines for the offerings to be buried with the ruler. Other workers were down at the river bank, digging clay with which to give the mound a smoothly finished coat.

Back in the village there was the cheerful noise of people at work. Down either side of an open stretch were uneven rows of skin-covered *tipis* and huts built of logs with clay and grass stuffed between the chinks. Open spaces separated the huts of the different clans. Lazy trails of smoke curled up from clay-lined fireplaces scooped out of the ground, where various dinners bubbled away in cooking pots tended by old women and watched hopefully by dogs of different sizes and colors.

As Eric strolled down the central pathway between the houses, he thought to himself that Mound Village women were not very neat about their house cleaning. Broken pieces of pottery, bones picked clean by the dogs, and other litter lay on the ground. One woman was tidying around her doors by spreading layers of fresh dirt on top of everything else, a method of house cleaning much appreciated by archaeologists who came along hundreds of years afterwards.

In a vacant space between two huts a group of boys were pitching water-worn stones shaped like biscuits. One boy proudly showed his friends a large new stone marble, beautifully carved. Though Eric towered above even the tallest of the boys, they were sturdy and well built, with bronze skins, prominent noses, and straight black hair above dark eyes slanted slightly upward.

Young children, naked except for their bead necklaces, rolled happily on the ground, playing with the puppies. The older people Eric met wore little clothing; there were brightly colored loincloths for the men and apronlike skirts for the women, and they generally adorned themselves with several strings of bead necklaces and copper bracelets. Male and female alike wore earplugs in the lobes of their ears.

Strolling on to the river terrace below the hill, Eric saw a number of women and girls working in a large garden where tall cornstalks stood in rows, their tassels waving in the breeze like the feather headdresses of warriors. Corn was a new and highly interesting food to Eric. He planned to carry some of it home, if he ever got home again. Beans twined up the cornstalks. Between the rows were the large green leaves of squash plants and pumpkin vines. One woman was cultivating a patch of tobacco with a hoe made from the shoulder blade of a deer set in a wooden handle. Another was digging around the corn with a mussel-shell hoe. Looking beyond the garden patch, Eric saw men in a boat on the river. One was standing with his spear poised, ready to spear a fish in a fish trap made of stakes driven across the river bed.

A shout drew Eric's attention back to the village. People were running from all sides to gather around a party of hunters who were bringing in a bear which they had caught in a trap. Two others carried a deer slung on a pole, a broken-off spear shaft

dangling from its side. One small hunter held up a new bow and arrow in one hand, proudly displaying a rabbit in the other. The hunters threw themselves down to rest, leaving the women to skin the animals. Later the skins would be scraped and treated with ashes and bark brews to make them soft and beautiful.

When the excitement had died down, the people drifted back to work, but Eric continued with his walk. He paused to watch several women who were weaving cloth at small looms. An older woman was carefully knotting thread into a net to be used in trapping fish. Several girls spinning fibers of nettles, grass, fur, and hair into yarns for the weavers followed the tall and fair-skinned stranger with their merry black eyes.

In front of the largest house in the village Eric saw a knot of women looking at a length of cloth that had just been taken from the loom. It was a thick, finely woven piece of considerable size, made from the fiber of milkweed. It was to be used as a shroud for the great chieftain who had just died. As the women fingered and admired it, neither they nor Eric could have dreamed that, centuries later, a piece of this burial cloth would be discovered by archaeologists. It was preserved by the chemical action of the two large copper breastplates in which the dead chieftain was laid to rest.

In the house of the dead chief, treasures were being collected for the burial. Eric saw bracelets and breastplates of shining copper and earplugs covered with thinly beaten silver. There were many necklaces of fresh-water pearls. Hundreds of other pearls were sewed on the chief's burial cape, along with sparkling mica cutouts of human hands and of bird claws. Eric saw a young warrior look wistfully at the chieftain's great headdress, a beautiful helmet of copper set with pearls.

Elsewhere the priests of the tribe were gathering together ceremonial offerings to go into the grave. They had collected large knife blades of obsidian, or volcanic glass, from the faraway

Yellowstone, spear points of quartz, an enormous ceremonial copper ax, and little baked clay figures of men and women.

All over the village and in other villages as well, Eric knew, craftsmen were hurriedly finishing offerings to go into the mound with the dead chief. He stopped to watch an artist carve a stone tobacco pipe made in the shape of a bird. Nearby were other pipes

MOUND BUILDER ART
Left, engraved stone disk; center, engraved shell gorget;
right, carved stone pipe

representing dogs, hawks, raccoons, and other animals sacred to the different clans. Potters surrounded by rolls of soft clay were making funeral bowls, vases, dishes, cups, and bottles. The best artists of the tribe were cutting designs of birds and flowers on pottery pieces already baked. Meanwhile the hunters were preparing weapons—flint scrapers, knives, and hammers—for the dead chief to carry into the spirit world.

Eric returned to his hut to eat but not to sleep. The noise and excitement of the day carried far into the night, making sleep impossible. The following day, many people gathered to pay their tribute to the dead chief. Everyone spoke of his skill in oratory, of the manner in which he had settled the disputes that had arisen from time to time among the leaders of the many tribes of the confederacy. During his time things had gone well; people had not fought among themselves. Traders had been able to make long journeys to distant places to bring back treasures in exchange for pottery and other objects made by the local craftsmen. As they worked, the artists and the craftsmen spoke among themselves of how well things had gone for them during the time of this ruler; they had been free to study and work, to invent new things, and to study the crafts of other tribes.

There was sadness over the death of such a great leader, but there was also a great deal of talk about what would happen now. Who could really take his place? Now this man and now that one was mentioned, but no one seemed fit to step into the place of the dead man; none was as good at oratory, as skillful at settling disputes, as encouraging to the artists and the craftsmen as the leader who was dead. Eric could understand much that he heard. During the years he had lived here he had come to know much about the language, life, and customs of these people. Now they no longer seemed as strange and as savage as he had at first thought them.

In spite of himself, Eric was impressed with the ceremonies that followed: the burning of the dead chief, the placing of treasures in the vault, and the construction of the mound over his remains. Not everything was strange. Eric's own Viking ancestors had burned a dead ruler in his beached ship, surrounded by his possessions, and then had piled earth and stones on top to make a monument.

But the dances! Did these people never sleep? It seemed to Eric that the ceremonies went on forever—the lines of brightly costumed dancers weaving back and forth in the firelight, the rites that were performed on the ramps of the tall pyramids, the smoky torches that sent a flickering light over the priests in their paint and feathers and glittering costumes sewed with pearls and sparkling mica, the endless chants and songs, the oratory. No one could have imagined such things, thought Eric.

EVIDENCES OF MOUND BUILDER LIFE. We have not merely imagined this story of a Viking in a Mound village. Every word of it is based on the patient work of many archaeologists, who spent hot months digging into the thousands of mounds that rise along the branches of the Mississippi and the Ohio rivers. You can read their accounts in the books listed at the end of this volume. The sound and color, poetry and oratory of the Mound Builders vanished long before our own forefathers came to this country. But in these crumbled mounds their art objects have remained.

The mounds are found in almost all the valleys of the Mississippi and the Ohio river systems. We may be sure that they were not piled up without public ceremonies in mind and that the splendid pearl-sewn robes and copper headdresses found in them were used in impressive rites. The great talent shown in Iroquois and other Indian oratory, poetry, and political organization is evidence of an earlier culture, for such abilities do not appear suddenly but are the outgrowth of centuries of ceremonial life.

TYPES OF MOUNDS. North America's mounds were of many shapes and must have been used in several ways. Some of the mounds built in the lower Mississippi at about the time of Columbus towered eighty feet high and were two hundred feet square at the base. Some were piled up to serve as the bases for temples. Others were enormous earth sculptures used as sites for religious rituals. Many were burial places for great chiefs or priests. The most common form was that of a pyramid with a flat top upon which altars or temples must have been built. Unluckily, the temples were not built of stone but probably of wood, which rots in damp valleys and forests and thus disappears. The idea of flat-topped pyramids may have come in from Mexico or Yucatán, to spread from the Mississippi to the Ohio area.

The mounds used as burial places were often cone-shaped. The evidence makes it clear that the bodies of chiefs and priests were laid underneath a framework covered by thatch, which was then set on fire to burn the body. Finally, an earth mound was piled above the treasures placed with the honored remains.

Many mounds had geometric forms, the most common of which was a great circle with a square on one side and a smaller circle on the other. In a grouping of this type found in Ross County, Ohio, more than two hundred burials were made.

The earth sculptures, or "effigy" mounds, were in the shape of snakes, alligators, turtles, birds, and even men. Perhaps the most famous of those that you may see today is the Great Serpent Mound of southern Ohio. Here earth was piled up to form an enormous serpent, over thirteen hundred feet long from the head to the coiled tail. Open jaws seem on the point of swallowing a small egg-shaped mound. The serpent and the egg undoubtedly were the symbols of life and creation to the builders of this mound, as they have been to many other people. We can be quite sure that such effigy mounds were used as the sites for religious ceremonies.

Another famous example of the work of the Mound Builders is the Great Mound which Qn Eric visited. It is sometimes called the Grave Creek Mound and is near the present town of Moundsville, West Virginia. This is one of the highest cone-shaped mounds in the United States. Yet it is only one of several large mounds in an area stretching ten or twelve miles along the banks of the Ohio.

The Great Mound was built long before the time of Columbus. When West Virginia was settled, this mound was already thickly

covered over with large trees. When in 1828 one white oak growing on top of the mound was cut, it was found, by counting the
growth rings, to be five hundred years old. Since these trees must
have sprouted after the mound had been abandoned, the Great
Mound may have been last used by its makers before 1328.

The Great Mound was opened in 1838 by curious people who
unfortunately were not trained for this work, as anthropologists
are now. Workers dug a horizontal tunnel from the north end of
the mound toward its center. About one hundred feet in, they
came to a vault some eight by twelve feet in area and seven feet
high. The vault had once been lined with timbers at the sides and
top, but this wood had long since rotted and caved in. Beneath
the debris of the roof were several human skeletons, hundreds of
beads made of sea shells, and various Indian objects such as those
we talked about in Eric's story.

A shaft ten feet wide was sunk from the top of the mound, and
a second vault was discovered. It was directly over the first and
was of the same size. From this upper mound the searchers took
more human bones, over seventeen hundred beads, five hundred
sea shells, five copper bracelets, and many pieces of mica. They
also found a flat stone inscribed with what looked like Viking
runes. This stone has caused a great deal of argument. No one can
be sure whether the stone was actually found inside the vault or
whether it had been placed there as a joke by some of the diggers.
Though various people have made what they call translations of
this Grave Creek tablet, it is the present opinion of the archaeologists of the National Museum in Washington that the stone was
planted in the excavation by a trickster.

MOUND BUILDER ART. Basketmaker Pueblo records were preserved by the dry air and sand of the Southwest, but most of the
story of the Mound Builders has been swallowed up by the damp
forests and river bottoms. Little more than the thousands of stone
and clay objects taken from the mounds remains to tell us about

life along the Mississippi and Ohio as it was during the age of the Viking explorers.

Almost all of what we know about Mound Builders comes from offerings placed in the graves of rulers and priests. The most common objects found were stone pipes, some well over a foot long. Since they weighed up to eighteen pounds, they must have been smoked with the bowl resting on the ground. Such pipes were probably used as a part of religious, social, or political ceremonies. Carved stone pipes are found by the dozens in Ohio and the Great Lakes region. The animal forms most popular were dogs, bears, wolves, and members of the cat family. Perhaps these were the symbols of the different clans. Pipes carved in the shape of ducks, owls, hawks, eagles, and other birds are also fairly common.

Pottery was made in the form of animal effigy jars. One pottery jar from a mound in Tennessee represents a dog with a curly tail. Other jars show different animals, such as frogs, fish, and birds. One remarkable jar shows a human head and another shows a hunchback. These were found in Arkansas.

Stone images of human beings were less common. They were made in a region about five hundred miles long, centering in western Tennessee. These images were usually buried in stone boxes in pairs, a male and a female. No one knows why. They may have been idols or the images of dead chiefs and their wives.

The area near Hopewell, Ohio, may have been the capital of a loosely organized confederacy of tribes living on the central plains drained by the Mississippi River system.

The graves of Hopewell rulers, such as the one Eric saw in our imaginary story, contained treasures that marked the buried men as chiefs of considerable power and wealth. Some of these treasures came from distant places. It is thought that each town may have had its own chiefs and priests but that there must have been some kind of federated government to keep peace and encourage trade among the various tribes over this area. Perhaps the tribes sent members to a central council which met from time to time. Democratic government did not come to the New World only with the white man; the Indians had used it all over the Americas.

EXTENT OF MOUND BUILDER COMMERCE. In order to get the things they wanted, the Mound Builders must have traded with distant tribes or sent out exploring parties. They obtained copper from the Lake Superior region, where there were pure nuggets soft enough to be worked without smelting. The Indians who mined copper made tools, weapons, and ornaments of it. A few hundred miles away, copper was used only for art and adornment. Farther away, it became a rare metal sacred to rulers and priests.

Most other regions had treasures useful for trading purposes. Atlantic, Pacific, and Gulf tribes dealt in sea shells used for gorgets, or necklace ornaments, in shark's teeth, and in other prizes. Inland tribes searched river banks for fresh-water pearls, thousands of which were sewed on the Mound Builders' clothing. Mica from the mines of Virginia and North Carolina was highly valued for cutout ornaments. Quartz and other minerals came from the mountains. Rocks rolled smooth by northern glaciers were made into stone axes. Mound Builder bands may have gone to the Yellowstone area for grizzly-bear teeth, and to volcanic deposits of the West for obsidian with which to make ritual knives.

Objects made in the Hopewell area were traded over a wide territory. Their beauty and careful workmanship also suggest that there were special groups of craftsmen and artists who were trained by some system such as that of the craft guilds of Medieval Europe. The enormous mounds tell us that there must have been some form of government powerful enough to direct the cooperative work of large numbers of people.

MAYAN INFLUENCE? The Mound Builders left no written records. One way to learn about such people is to study their living descendants, but no one knows what happened to the descendants of the Mound Builders. Although these people left no records behind them, the objects found in their mounds make it seem likely that there was a close connection between them and some of the tribes of Central America.

A good many of the art objects found in Mound Builder sites are strikingly like those made by the Mayas of southern Mexico and Yucatán. A pipe from southern Ohio, made in the form of a human being, the pipe mouthpiece on his headdress and the bowl between his feet, looks very much like Mayan art. The design on a plate unearthed at Etowah, Georgia, is almost identical with those of faraway Mexico. A large stone disk, used by a Mound Builder artist as a palette for mixing his paint, is almost exactly like art objects made in Yucatán. These clues are very strong in the Mississippi region where the temple mounds are most thickly scattered. They grow more faint as one moves northward into the Great Lakes area.

No one knows how the Mound Builders came into contact with Mayan art objects. Perhaps a band of Mayas came by boat across the Gulf of Mexico to the mouth of the Mississippi after hard times fell on the so-called first Mayan empire, about the eighth century after Christ. On the other hand, a few Mayan art objects might have been passed from hand to hand to reach the United States area, although this would not explain why the clues suddenly appear so thickly in the lower Mississippi area.

How the Mound Builder Culture Developed. No one knows exactly how the Mound Builder culture came about. A long time before these people made their great mounds, wandering tribes of hunters settled down in the Mississippi and Ohio valleys. The use of corn probably reached this area some centuries after it had come to the Southwest. The making of mounds was begun some time in the ninth century, perhaps after Mayan ideas had seeped into our country. From the Mound Builder center near Hopewell, Ohio, ideas and art forms spread to country that is now Michigan,

Pennsylvania, New York, Tennessee, Indiana, Illinois, Wisconsin, Iowa, Kansas, and even as far south as Florida. Mound Builder culture reached its highest development between the ninth and the fourteenth centuries.

Here is a skeleton chart that shows how these people changed from century to century, together with the names which archaeologists give to the various periods of their development.

PERIOD	DATE	CULTURE
Archaic Period	500 B.C. — 500 A.D.	People were hunters and food collectors. Spear throwers were used. They had no farming, cloth making, or pottery.
Burial Mound I	500 — 900 A.D.	New: Burial mounds and villages were built. They made pottery and woven articles. Tobacco pipes were made. Some farming began.
Burial Mound II	900 — 1300 A.D.	New: Large burial mounds were built. Art forms developed. Wide trade with distant tribes.
Temple Mound I	1300 — 1500 A.D.	New: Pyramids and art forms suggesting Mexican or Mayan influence. Buffalo hunting organized.
Temple Mound II	1500 — 1700 A.D.	City-states flourished in the middle Mississippi area, then came to some unknown end.

THE END OF THE MOUND BUILDERS. The Mound Builders had come to an unknown end before the first white settlers appeared in their area. Were they destroyed by wandering tribes? Did the corn crops fail them when there were no good areas left to burn

over and grass had taken their fields? Was there some weather
change that affected them?

Students have suggested that the Mound Builders may have
given up agriculture and turned to buffalo hunting after an
increase of those herds in the southern area. If so, they may have
become wanderers themselves and followed the buffalo into
extinction.

A historian has his tools just as an archaeologist does, and such
tools include the science of asking the right questions when con-
fronted with a mystery. If we apply the yardsticks which the
English historian Toynbee has furnished us, we may summarize
the mystery of the Mound Builder culture in somewhat the following way. Their culture developed out of an archaic period
around 500 A.D. and received some new stimulus, expressed in fine
arts and extensive temple building, around 900 A.D. There is evidence that this stimulus came from the Mexica-Mayan culture of
Central America, though it is not clear as yet how this contact
came about.

The challenge the Mound Builders met was that of flood and
forest and pressure from nomadic tribes. From the evidence, it
may be that their answer to this challenge was the creation of
many city-states, banded together in a political confederacy which
represented the "Universal State" and which, according to Toynbee, usually appears near the end of a civilization. Owing to the
absence of written records, we know nothing of the political ideas
or the philosophy or the religion which this culture produced,
though we may make certain guesses about them on the basis of
historical evidence about the Iroquois and other tribes of later
days, whose political and oratorical skills were not those of crude
savages.

The Mound Builder time of trouble came before the appearance
of our own ancestors. Their culture fell into complete decline
under the stress of some combination of trials which may have

included nomadic raids, internal political troubles, and some change in their food production. Perhaps grass choked out their cornfields. Exhausted soil and sudden disease may have played a part in their decline. Such hypotheses may be investigated by those who study the silent burial mounds. Other hypotheses would be less easy to check; perhaps the effort the Mound Builders had expended to conquer the Mississippi and the Ohio river systems and to weld a political organization had exhausted their creative energies in a climate which discouraged great effort during much of the year. We know, too, that the Mound Builders put up a great many temple mounds. It may be that their leaders of later days were priests who turned to religious mysticism and neglected the political and physical efforts necessary to defend their culture from the attacks of sturdy and envious hunting tribes who pressed on the fringes of the Mound Builder culture.

Such hypotheses may or may not be proved correct, but there is only one way that the true story of the Mound Builders will ever be known, and that is by a continuation of the patient study of the hundreds of mounds which dot the banks of the Mississippi and the Ohio river systems.

VIII. THE WARRIOR DEMOCRACIES OF THE EASTERN FORESTS

To the Lynx

(FROM AN OSAGE INVOCATION TO THE SACRED ANIMALS)

What shall the little ones make to be their symbol of courage, as they
    travel the path of life? it has been said, in this house.
The little mottled lynx that lies outstretched, they said,
He who is their grandfather, a person of great courage, they shall make
    to be their symbol of courage, it has been said, in this house.
At break of day
My grandfather (the lynx) rushed forth to attack
A deer with curved horns.
My grandfather struck the deer and made it lie outstretched in death.
My grandfather approached the fallen deer
With an air of exultation;
He gave a cry of triumph and spake, saying:
When, towards the setting sun the little ones
Go forth to strike the enemy,
In this very manner they shall always triumph.
Their hands shall ever be upon the foe, as they travel the path of life.
Here he made a curve, it has been said, in this house.

As time passed, the Indian magic songs used to help capture game
animals expanded into great religious poetry, full of beauty and meaning. This is part of a long Osage invocation to the sacred animals
thought to be patrons or ancestors of the different clans. These animals
were symbols of courage, strength, or fleetness. Here the lynx is the
"grandfather" from whom courage might be learned. This song, translated by Francis La Flesche, the Plains Indian anthropologist, describes
an example of man's age-old custom of identifying himself with animal
spirits thought to be ancestors of human beings.

THE WARRIOR DEMOCRACIES
OF THE EASTERN FORESTS

AT LEAST one Viking colony was frightened away from America by Indian warriors, the savage *skraelings* of the sagas. Our own ancestors who came here on the Mayflower found, however, that in their first winter friendly Indians saved them from starvation. Which picture of the Indians is true?

Both are true. Savage, painted warriors with tomahawks, skulking behind forest trees, wigwams, smoke signals, blood-chilling war cries, and the torture of prisoners—this is one side of the picture. Friendly Indians bringing gifts of corn and turkeys to starving white men; Aspinet the Nauset teaching the Puritans to plant corn and pumpkins; Pocahontas of Virginia saving the life of Captain John Smith; Hiawatha, the great orator of the Iroquois League of Six Nations—this is another side.

In 1492 the ancestors of Aspinet and Pocahontas were living in the eastern forests much as their own ancestors had lived for hundreds of years before them. The Indians of the eastern forests were not city dwellers, but neither were they the crude savages that later white settlers thought them. No great civilization developed in the eastern forests. Men with nothing better than stone axes cannot clear land easily. Farming was more difficult in this northeastern area, where winters were long, than it was in warmer parts of the Americas. Then, too, the constant supply of game made farming less necessary.

The ancient history of the eastern woodland area is less well known than that of other parts of our country because the damp forests swallowed up the Indian villages and the art objects made of wood. Altars, huts, canoes, baskets, boxes, and other wooden objects have long since turned to dust. Only a few stone weapons and tools, bits of pottery and gorgets, finely carved pipes, and trumpets of shell have outlasted the centuries.

ANCIENT PREHISTORY OF THE EASTERN FORESTS. Their tools and weapons tell us that Folsom Man roamed the eastern coasts at a time when mastodons and mammoths still lived in the Americas. Thousands of years later, basketmaking Indians were there, hunting, fishing, and gathering seeds, nuts, and fruits. These hunters took shelter in caves and under rocky ledges, leaving behind them their tools and the bones of the animals they ate. They did not make pottery or pipes or ornaments and had not learned to plant crops or to bury their dead.

During prehistoric times many tribes, speaking many different languages, roamed the forests of eastern America. The Iroquois were a large group living in and around New York State. The Algonquin lived outside the Iroquois area throughout New England, the Great Lakes region, and down the Atlantic coast as far as North Carolina. Other tribes were distributed through the more southerly areas.

Ancient shell heaps along the Atlantic coast from Canada to Florida show us where some of the tribes lived in early days. The early northern tribes did not bury objects with their dead, but well-made stone axes, gouges, and pestles are found in their refuse heaps. Long before the Vikings came, Indians along the South Atlantic coast began to bury their dead in urns, to put small figures into the graves, and to make pottery and carved shell and stone objects.

By 500 A.D. the idea of corn planting had reached the Atlantic seaboard. Later the Indians there cultivated squash, beans, and other plants. The corn growers found time to make objects for use in religious rites, to shape clay into pots and bowls, and to build mounds with altars on them.

By 900 A.D. farming was fairly common and people had even more time for politics and religion. New ideas and customs came in from mound-building Indians of the Mississippi area. By 1300 A.D. the eastern forest Indians were making artistic pottery, ornaments, pipes, and other objects.

Their villages were on hilltops, and the wooden walls which often surrounded them suggest that the tribes fought among themselves over hunting areas. Behind the palisades, village life went on in well-organized ways. Beside the bark-covered houses were garden patches. There were meeting places for religious and social ceremonies. Dogs ran in and out. Women tended crops with spadelike tools of bone or wood. They cultivated corn, squash, sunflowers, tobacco, pumpkins, and beans. Corn seed was planted in hills, and in some places manure or a dead fish was buried with the grain. Squash and beans twined around the cornstalks. In colder regions where corn could not flourish, there was no farming. In the warmer southern areas, other foods were grown in addition to "the three sisters," as the Indians called corn, beans, and squash. These were millet, melons, sweet potatoes, gourds, and tobacco. Indians of the North made maple sugar from the sap of the maple tree.

Women were skillful at weaving baskets, dressing skins, embroidering costumes with porcupine quills and bits of fur, or patting coils of clay into pots and jars. Men made bows and arrows and spears, hunted and fished, and took part in the religious rituals. The tribes of the South made beautiful wood carvings, but few of these escaped destruction by rot or fire.

The life of these people of the Atlantic seaboard in pre-Columbian days was probably not very different from the life of later white people in the same area. It centered around the temple which was their church, and the chief's house which was their courthouse. They spent their time in hunting, fishing, and food

gathering, and these tasks were spiced with activities not unlike the cornhuskings, revival meetings, feuds, and log raising of the rural South of later days.

THE IROQUOIS. The Iroquois roamed the eastern woodlands in 1492 and were still very much on the scene when the Pilgrims settled at Plymouth in 1620. These tribes became the bitter enemies of French settlers and their Indian allies, the Hurons. Early French missionaries described the Iroquois as savages of the lowest order who tortured prisoners and practiced cannibalism. Certainly the Iroquois, when on the warpath, scalped their enemies and forced their prisoners to run the gantlet between two rows of women and children provided with whips, clubs, and knives. But Iroquois cannibalism was ceremonial. It was based on the belief that by eating the flesh of a brave warrior who had died under torture, living men would take the dead warrior's courage.

In their homes the Iroquois were remarkable for good humor, generosity, and intelligence. They showed a great talent for oratory, poetry, and political organization.

At the time America was discovered, the Iroquois lived in permanent villages in cleared parts of the northeastern forests. Each family group farmed a plot of land, usually given over to corn, beans, squash, and tobacco.

Iroquois houses were rectangular lodges from fifty to a hundred feet long, built of wooden poles covered with bark. Each lodge was divided into a number of stalls where different families lived, four families using the same fire pit. Along the walls of each stall were bunks for sleeping. From the rafters hung strips of corn, dried pumpkins, and squash.

These houses belonged to the women. A man lived in the house of his wife as long as they got along well together, but when trouble arose, it was the husband who left and went home to his mother's house. Home life among the Iroquois, as early white observers reported it, was notable for its unfailing courtesy and kindness. The Iroquois, like most of the other Indians, were horrified to discover that white people struck their children. Though Iroquois children were given much freedom, were seldom punished and never whipped, it is said that they were docile and obedient. Unfortunately, no one has made it clear how Iroquois parents accomplished this remarkable feat of child training.

Kinship in the family group might be by adoption, but whether by blood or adoption, descent was counted through the mother's line. Such a system is called a "matriarchy." Under it, a man belonged to the clan of his mother, never to that of his father or of his wife. The oldest matron of the ruling family of the tribe had a position of great influence, and her views were of the utmost importance when the time came to choose a new chief.

The most remarkable political achievement of the Iroquois was the League of Six Nations, which was formed about 1570, some seventy-eight years after Columbus discovered America. After a long period of tribal warfare over the rich lands of central New York, certain Iroquois chiefs had come to see that, in the long run, everyone benefits by peace.

Among the founders of this League were the Mohawks, Oneidas, Senecas, Cayugas, and Onondagas; in later days new tribes were taken into it, some of whom did not speak the Iroquois language. Fifty sachems or wise men served on the council of the League. When one sachem died, another chief from the same tribe replaced him. This council regulated intertribal affairs of war and peace.

Hiawatha and Deganawida, according to Iroquois legends, were the great men who brought about this union of the Indian groups. Much Iroquois oratory praised the way the League safeguarded peace and happiness and instilled correct behavior, thought, and speech. These leaders were among the many excellent Iroquois orators; oratory was a necessary skill when a complete agreement of all chiefs was required for action. The Quakers, it has been said, borrowed this idea of complete agreement, instead of the majority rule more common among English-speaking people, from the Iroquois.

Little remains of this oratory. The Iroquois had no writing system, though public speeches and decisions and actions were recorded by means of white and purple beads in wampum belts, which served as memory aids to the men who memorized the history of the tribe and passed it on to the young. The few examples of oratory which have come down to us are evidence of the political skill and real wisdom of these men who were so feared by some of the white settlers.

One of the Iroquois prayers is not only Christian in feeling but is astonishingly like the "Hymn in Praise of All Created Things," written by Saint Francis of Assisi, the twelfth-century Italian saint who called all animals "brother." Here is a part of the Iroquois prayer:

Hail! Hail! Hail! Thou who hast created all things, who rulest all things, listen to our words. . . . Give to the keepers of the faith wisdom to execute properly thy command. . . .

We return thanks to our mother, the earth, which sustains us, that she has been caused to yield so plentifully of her fruits. . . .

We return thanks to all the herbs and plants of the earth;

We thank them for giving us strength to preserve our bodies in health and for curing us of the diseases inflicted upon us by evil spirits.

We return thanks to the Three Sisters, the main sustainers of our lives.

We return thanks to the bushes and the trees; we thank the winds which banish disease as they move.

We thank the thunderbirds who give us happiness and comfort by having the rain descend on the earth, causing all plants to grow.

We thank the moon and the stars and the sun. May the latter never hide his face from us in shame and leave us in darkness. . . .

The Iroquois resisted the white invasion longer than any other tribe did, but at last one of their leaders saw that the end of Iroquois freedom had come:

Once our fathers were strong and their power was felt throughout the land. But we have been reduced and broken by the cunning and the rapacity of the white-skinned race. Many winters ago our ancestors predicted that a great monster with white eyes would consume our land. This monster is the white race and the prediction is near its fulfillment. . . .

IX. FOOD GATHERERS OF THE FAR NORTH AND WEST

One Woman Paying Her Respects to Another

I recognized the poor Saatina
Who could not sing
I recognized the poor Saatina
Who could not make drum songs.
No, she was not such a one.
A right merry person,
A bright woman,
Who always sang on the island Aaluit,
Who always squalled with all her might.

This is a drum-contest song of the kind used by people of the Far North to vent their private antagonisms. A rule of "trial-by-poetry" contests was that insults should make onlookers laugh, such witty truthfulness being considered "good medicine" for the soul. Poor Saatina's rival jeers at her because, though she squalls with all her might, she cannot make good drum songs. We may be sure that Saatina retorted with a compliment in the same spirit.

These people also made up "death songs" which are sad and lovely. Here is one of them, from a Tlingit poet.

Song of Cgwᴀtc

I always think within myself
That there is no place
Where people do not die.

I do not know where my uncle is.
Probably the spirits threw down my uncle
Into the spirits' cave around this world.

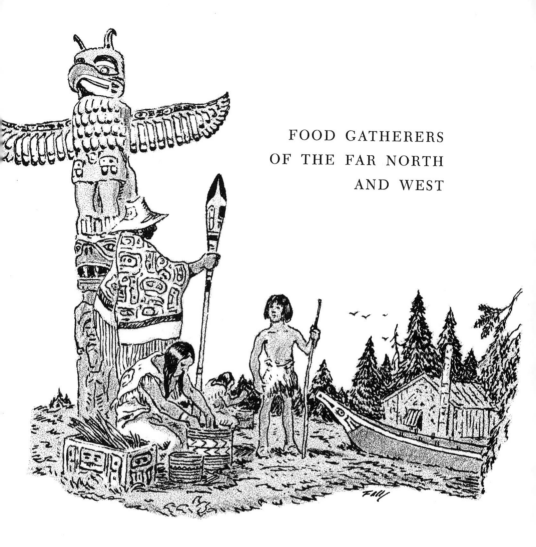

Although we are considering the people who lived in the Americas before the time of Columbus, and so do not attempt to tell much about what happened to the Indians after 1492, this does not mean that all the Indian societies you have been reading about have vanished, as have the Folsom hunters, the ancient Basketmakers, and the Mound Builders. A culture survives a much longer time than do any of the families of which it is composed. Many of the cultures of pre-Columbian America are still flourishing today. Any one of you who has lived or traveled in the Southwest knows that it is still Indian country in many sections. The Pueblo farmers, the Navaho shepherds, the Apaches, and the desert people still retain many of their ancient customs. Although the Indians of the Eastern forests were dispossessed of their lands and put on reservations, remnants of their cultures are still alive. Several countries of Central and South America are strongly Indian in population, and national figures in government and in the arts proudly speak of their Indian blood and heritage.

The map on page 12 shows where the pre-Columbian ancestors of many modern Indian groups established the settlements that are maintained to this day. Among these are the cultures we will discuss in this chapter: the Eskimo hunters of the Far North, the fishermen of the Northwest coast, and the seed gatherers of California.

If Qn Eric, that much-traveled legendary Viking, had wandered far north and west of Leif's camping place at New Brunswick, up into the northernmost part of America, he would have discovered the Arctic desert, the tundra, where long, dark, very cold winters are followed by short summers bright with the midnight sun. Here Eric would have found a people who call themselves simply "The People."

We call them Eskimos. By Viking times the Eskimos had already lived in their vast, treeless plain of ice and snow for a thousand years. As more Eskimo relics come to light, preserved by the frozen soil, their ancient history may be better known. Ancient traces of these people are found in widely scattered locations in Siberia, Alaska, and in the Hudson Bay region as far east as Greenland.

Today, a thousand years after the time of the Vikings, the Eskimos still live much as Eric would have found them. They are a merry, sociable people who settle their personal quarrels publicly by means of singing debates in which each contestant tries

to get the better of the other by wit and sarcasm. Although
Eskimo customs differ somewhat in various parts of their wide
area, the people are much alike wherever they are found and
speak a common language difficult for outsiders to learn.

Eskimo life depends largely upon caribou and fish. When the
caribou come north in summer, the Eskimos follow the migrating
herds from one feeding spot to another, killing the animals by
driving them into natural or artificial lanes where hunters are
hidden. Each day they skin the animals they have killed and
store the meat in a cache, a storage place under the earth, or
dry it on high poles out of reach of animals. During the long
winter nights Eskimo women cut and sew skins into close-fitting
coats and trousers and hoods.

When the caribou go south in winter, Eskimo men and boys
hunt seal and other sea food. They spear fish through holes in the

ice or from skin-covered boats called "kayaks." In the cold Arctic some of the Eskimos live in round igloos built of blocks of ice and warmed by blubber-burning lamp stoves. In warmer Alaska, however, they live in skin tents in the summer and in underground huts of driftwood and earth in the winter.

Since the Eskimos move about so much, their art objects must be small and portable. For centuries they have scratched designs on small, carved ivory objects. They also make grotesque masks for use in comic contests or in the magic rituals practiced to bring about good hunting.

THE FISHERMEN OF THE NORTHWEST COAST. Had Eric continued across the top of America, he would have come to the northwest coast of the Pacific, a strip of land in some ways like his own country. Here the coast line is cut by steep fiords. Mountain ranges covered with dense forests of fir, spruce, and cedar come almost to the sea. The warm Japan current flowing by causes a heavy rainfall, which makes the land rich in food plants and game. For untold centuries people have lived here, piling up shell-heap mounds beside the sites of their villages.

This rich land was always a melting pot where tribes from the interior of America mixed with others newly arrived from Asia. Thus the society which grew up here became a hodgepodge of customs and arts. Eric, whose own Viking ancestors had been given to boasting and telling tall tales during the feasts in the great halls, might have found these people somewhat like his own.

When it was first explored by white men some two centuries ago, this thousand-mile strip of wooded coast was the home of prosperous tribes of hunters and fishermen whose lives were probably not very different from those of the people who lived there before Columbus. When the salmon ran up the rivers to spawn, the tribes—with names like the Haida, the Chilcat, the Tlingit—gathered in temporary camps on the banks of the streams. With nets, harpoons, and fish traps they caught enormous numbers of salmon which they dried and smoked. At other seasons they collected roots, berries, and nuts, and hunted deer, elk, and bear. Then they retired for a winter of feasting and ceremony in permanent villages at the water's edge.

The social events of the Haida and Chilcat tribes took place, like those of the Vikings, in long wooden halls, which were usually distinguished by the tall totem poles standing in front of them. These totem poles, fashioned from tree trunks and carved and painted with a series of totem symbols—animals, perhaps, or plants or birds—signified the unity, equivalent to blood relationship, existing among groups of people who believed themselves to have an intimate relationship with some particular natural object or phenomenon. Some of these tribes developed a social system which reminds us somewhat of our own wealth-loving society. Their people were divided into three classes: the nobles, the common people, and the slaves. Nobility was not founded upon physical or mental or spiritual superiority, as was fairly usual among American Indians, but depended upon wealth and display. The ideal of the noble is expressed in one of their songs:

But he does not work and plan at all, the great real one, the great one whose voice is true.

The scorn which was heaped on the common people is shown by another song:

The little ones who do many kinds of work, the little ones who work hard, who make mistakes.
Coming from insignificant places in the world and who try now to go to high places.

In this atmosphere of competition and lack of community spirit, symbolic cannibalism is not surprising. Everything could be bought: wives, slaves, even a man's most valuable possession, his name. Wealth consisted of stamped copper disks, large carved and painted houses and totem poles, enormous carved boats, piles of furs, beautifully woven blankets and capes, and smaller carved wood objects.

Their houses were large rectangular structures, sometimes over five hundred feet long and sixty feet wide. Many families might live together in one such house, each family beside its own fireplace. Painted totem poles carved from cedar logs were put in front of the houses of the nobles. Designs carved on totem poles and woven on the blankets and capes showed the mythical ancestors claimed by the owner. These might be animal or human. They were not likenesses but magic symbols. They showed animals that looked as if they had been split and laid flat. Some parts of the animal were made very large and other parts left out altogether. The artist threw in a pair of eyes, perhaps, or a cross section of a hip joint in the corner of the design.

This type of art is called "conventional." Unlike representational art, which shows things as the artist sees them, conventional art follows certain formal rules or conventions, often centuries old. The making of masks for magic ceremonies, for instance, was

CARVED WOODEN MASKS OF THE NORTHWEST COAST
Left: winter dance mask, Nootka, Vancouver Island; center: Alaskan dance mask; right: ceremonial mask, Tsimshian, British Columbia.

a conventional art highly popular among these people. Women were not permitted to create designs using true life forms. Even the designs they followed in weaving had to be first painted on boards by men artists.

These people practiced a variety of crafts. To weave the famous Chilcat blankets or capes, women stripped cedar bark into fine strands which were used as warp on upright looms. The wool of mountain goats served as a filling to be woven in between the weighted warp strands. Another craft was the carving of wooden dishes and boxes. Objects of horn were also popular. Horn from mountain sheep and goats, softened by boiling, was pressed into wooden molds, in which it hardened into the desired form. Later it was carved and polished by means of stone tools. Such tools, made of a local variety jade called nephrite, are found in British Columbia.

These small arts were already flourishing when the Russians introduced iron into this region some two centuries ago. After this, the arts of the Haida and Tlingit tribes blossomed into strange new forms. With the use of iron tools they were able to construct much grander houses and canoes, elaborately carved and painted.

Although the Indians of the Northwest had always loved ostentation and display, these traits seemed to become exaggerated after the coming of the white man to America. Perhaps the display of individual power and wealth, which was so unlike the usual Indian character, was the response made by these tribes to the challenge of the white invader, a challenge which in most other cases destroyed the Indian's pride in himself and his confidence in his gods. One might go a bit further with speculation. Within historic times Japanese fishing craft have been blown to these shores; might it be that this strange culture was some accidental development of a seed from faraway Japan, with its powerful feudal nobility system and its emphasis upon the forms of personal pride which are called "face saving"?

THE INDIANS OF CALIFORNIA. Had Eric traveled on down the California coast he would have come to a people very different from the wealth-loving northwestern tribes. Once past the central basin of California, he would have found an area where broad, grassy valleys were dotted with oaks and chaparral. The people who lived in these valleys and along the coast were hunters and fishermen who stayed within their own hunting grounds. They were of many tribes. Even as late as the time of the Spanish Conquest, the California Indians spoke twenty-two quite different languages and even more dialects. Their lives were simple and their possessions few. Early observers described them as being hospitable, joyous, musical, merry as birds, and given to an endless round of song, dance, and religious ceremony.

Shellfish mounds prove that their simple village life was very ancient, going back many hundreds of years. Folsom hunters had lived here when what is now desert land was fertile, with rivers and lakes. Other hunters, using stone weapons like those found in Gypsum Cave, Nevada, had also visited California, perhaps in search of obsidian.

These shell heaps tell of thousands of years of human life here, going back many centuries before the time of Christ. Household objects found in the heaps show little development from the oldest ones on the bottom layer to the latest on the top; for some reason these people never seemed to make much progress. Perhaps this was because there were no great canyons or hidden valleys in California into which unwarlike people could retreat. Wave after wave of invaders washed over this area. The variety of skull types, tools, and languages shows that the settlements were never free from invasion long enough for the arts and crafts to reach a high stage of development. Or perhaps the lack of a higher culture among the California tribes may have been caused by the lack of a rich food supply. These tribes had no domesticated animals. They did not have enormous herds of game animals to hunt, nor did they have the rich salmon rivers of the Northwest. Corn, which in the South and Southwest was creating a race of builders and conquerors, did not reach California. People living on seeds, roots, acorns, herbs, fish, and small game may not have an excess of energy with which to build cities or to defend themselves from warlike nomads.

For thousands of years the Indians of this region lived chiefly on acorns. These were made into an acorn flour that was cooked as mush or baked into cakes. Acorns were stored in basketry bins until they were needed, at which time they were pounded into flour. The tannic acid was dissolved out of the acorn flour by means of hot water.

The flour was boiled into mush in closely woven baskets in which water was heated by means of hot stones dropped in from time to time. Baskets and stirring spoons were the chief art products of these acorn-eating tribes. They did not develop pottery or textiles. Their clothes varied from stripes of paint to garments of deerskin. Their houses were simple shelters of bark or reeds. They had no great religious architecture.

Long after the Spanish Conquest, and in fact until today, the descendants of these people continued to make woven and twined baskets for acorn storage, cookery, and baby carrying.

SUMMARY. Back in the days when you could not telephone China and say that you would be there by the week end, it was really true, as a famous geologist liked to put it, that "you are what you are because you are where you are." In this chapter we have traced several groups in their responses to the world about them and have seen how different one group of people becomes from others simply because of the place in which it lives. Of these cultures, the oldest was that of the Eskimo, whose ancestors some thousands of years ago chose to remain in the cold north region near the Bering gateway, meeting the challenge of cold, fog, snow, and winter-long darkness by remarkable inventions: well-tailored and waterproof fur suits, the snow house and the blubber-burning lamp, the dog sled and the skin kayak. We have seen, too, that the Eskimos paid a price for this effort, in that their culture did not develop into a civilization but has remained unchanged for many hundreds of years.

It is interesting to compare the Eskimo with the seed gatherers of California, who lived in a country famous for its warmth, sunshine, and variety of plant foods. These basketmaking people were not driven by hunger to domesticate animals or plant crops, but lived an almost hand-to-mouth existence, feeding on acorns, pine nuts, grass seeds, roots, fish, rabbit, deer, and so forth. In this case, the absence of strong stimulus, and the time-consuming nature of seed gathering, may have hindered the development of a civilization. In a country famous today for its variety of religious cults, no great Indian religion developed; though shellfish deposits show that people lived there for thousands of years, there is little evidence of development in arts and crafts during this period.

The fishermen of the Northwest coast are interesting to us for another reason. Living on a strip of coastland where game and berries abounded, beside a sea swarming with fish, they had no problem of food supply. Responding to this lavish land, they built gaudy houses and boats and totem poles of the giant cedars, and feasted and bragged on a grand scale, inventing social and religious rites that remind us somewhat of Hollywood productions. Like the superior people shown in our magazine advertisements, they had everything material, and they made sure that everyone knew about it. In short, their puzzling resemblance to ourselves, combined with the fact that their culture does not seem to be a very old one, suggests that this display was stimulated by the appearance of strangers with a competing culture. Their emphasis upon the wealth and superiority of the individual, so unlike the usual Indian emphasis upon the value of the tribe, gave rise to interesting arts and crafts, but in their culture the human spirit did not rise to great heights. Despite their insistence on superiority and the abundance of their resources, their population has fallen from some sixty thousand people at the time of their discovery to a present twenty thousand.

X. THE MAYAN TRIUMPH AND FAILURE

Mayan Prophetic Chant

Eat, eat, while there is bread,
Drink, drink, while there is water;
A day comes when dust shall darken the air,
When a blight shall wither the land,
When a cloud shall arise,
When a mountain shall be lifted up,
When a strong man shall seize the city,
When ruin shall fall upon all things,
When the tender leaf shall be destroyed,
When eyes shall be closed in death;
When there shall be three signs on a tree,
Father, son and grandson hanging dead on the same tree;
When the battle flag shall be raised,
And the people scattered abroad in the forests.

Like Old Testament prophets, the Mayan and Mexican poet-priests foresaw the day of destruction for their people, and seldom has prophecy been more closely followed by disaster. The Mayan pre-Columbian prophet, Balam, told about the future coming of strangers with a new religion; his prophecies are gathered together in the *Books of Chilam Balam*. Spanish priests, true to the prophecy, tried to destroy the Mayan religion by destroying all the sacred books. Fortunately, an unknown Maya, shortly after the Conquest, wrote down Mayan legends in his own language but with the Spanish alphabet, and a later Spanish priest translated them into Spanish, giving us the best record of Mayan religious legends and poetry.

THE MAYAN TRIUMPH AND FAILURE

THE AMERICA THAT COLUMBUS FAILED TO DISCOVER. On his fourth and last voyage across the Sea of Darkness, Christopher Columbus made an unlucky decision which was to cost him the discovery of treasures greater than any that Europeans had ever wrested from the fabulous East. This decision was particularly unlucky because Columbus was in disfavor with the rulers of Spain: the great admiral had made an unsuccessful administrator of the islands he had discovered and had been forbidden to return to them, though he had at last been permitted to make another attempt to find the straits that he still believed must lead through the New World to India. Here is the story.

It had been a long and difficult voyage. Near Santo Domingo, where he had first planted the Spanish flag, Columbus sensed the approach of a tropical storm. He asked the governor of Santo Domingo to permit him to bring his ships into the harbor, but permission was refused. Then Columbus was forced to ride out the storm at sea, and when the hurricane passed, his four ships were battered and crippled.

Land lay ahead, but it was low and unpromising and it stretched off to a flat horizon. No need to look there for the long-desired straits leading to lands of spices and jewels.

After they had sailed on for some distance, the lookout on the flagship shouted, "Ship ahoy!"

The Spaniards, crowding to the rails, saw a strange sight below them. Twenty people were sitting in a dugout canoe eight feet wide. They were small, dark men with straight black hair. From his seat underneath a canopy their chieftain rose, laid his hand on his heart, and spoke what was clearly a welcome, though in a language that none of the Europeans could understand.

"Who are you and where do you come from?" the white men asked, in the various languages they spoke.

At last the dark chieftain seemed to understand their question. Pointing to the west, he repeated over and over again the two unfamiliar words, "Maiam" and "Yucatán." As he spoke, he made gestures that were clearly an invitation to visit his country.

Columbus, knowing his homesick sailors were on the verge of mutiny, shook his head and sailed eastward—to storm, mutiny, and death in disfavor. The Mayan chieftain returned home to Yucatán, doubtless to startle his hearers with incredible stories of the great ships with enormous wings.

On the day when Columbus met the Mayas, the cities of their ancestors were already in ruins, overgrown by the jungles of Guatemala and Honduras. The story of the greatest Indian civilization had already passed through three stages: the pre-Mayan era in which a corn culture was developed and astronomical studies begun, the Old Mayan era of magnificent temple building, and the dark age of the decline of this civilization. Its later rebirth in Yucatán was even then in decline.

DATING THE MAYAN ERAS. The story of the Mayas began at least three thousand years before Christ in what is now southern Mexico, Guatemala, and Honduras. A carving found near Vera Cruz, Mexico, carries a Mayan hieroglyphic date which is read as November 4, 291 B.C., while a statuette found near Tuxtla, in this same region, carries a date which corresponds to May 16, 98 B.C. These carvings are of the Old Mayan era, sometimes referred to as the "Old Empire," though the Mayas did not ever form an empire but, like the early Greeks, were a loosely related group of tribes living in independent city-states, but having languages, ancestors, arts, and sciences in common. By 317 A.D. Mayan priests and overlords were ruling vast agricultural districts from sacred centers whose temples of stucco and stone are among the world's most fascinating examples of architecture. The greatest period of Mayan art and architecture lasted from 472 A.D. to 620 A.D.; at almost exactly the time of the Fall of Rome and the beginning of the Dark Ages in Europe, the Old Mayan period went into a decline which lasted until about 980 A.D. By this time provincial towns in Yucatán were becoming quite prosperous, and by the tenth century the New Mayan era was in full swing, blending the Old Mayan culture with that of Toltec invaders from central Mexico. Civil wars weakened the New Mayan city-states after 1200, and the civilization was already in decline before the white invaders finished it off after 1517.

After Columbus the buried Mayan cities slept beneath the jungle for more than three hundred years. In 1839 President Martin Van Buren sent John L. Stephens to study the possibility of building a canal across Nicaragua to connect the Atlantic and Pacific oceans. Mr. Stephens did not get the canal route, but for

$50 cash he bought the old Mayan city of Copán. Here were the ruins of a once great city, designed and built by engineers and architects of great skill. Magnificent temples, palaces, and public buildings had towered above the tallest trees. Streets and courts had been paved with stone or cement; covered canals and underground sewers for drainage had been constructed of the same materials. Painted scenes adorned the interior walls of the temples, carved figures the outside. Hieroglyphs cut in the stone gave mute and baffling evidence of records and history.

This mysterious city now overgrown by jungle had clearly once been a great trading center. Pottery shards found in Copán now prove that there was commerce between Copán and cities of Mexico at a time when our own English ancestors were still living in lake dwellings, not dreaming of the Roman conquest to come.

The discovery of Copán buried in the deep jungle set the archaeological world on fire with questions. Who had left these enormous carved stones? When had this city flourished? How did these people get their start? To answer these questions, archaeologists have tried for a century to decipher Mayan hieroglyphs, have delved into ancient mounds and sorted out thousands upon thousands of Mayan relics.

Anthropologists believe that the early Mayas were among the most intelligent of earth's children. Old World civilizations were based on the utilization of wheat, rice, barley, sheep, pigs, cattle, oxen, and horses, as well as on the use of iron for tools and weapons. The Mayas had none of these. They had no advanced neighbors from whom they might have learned the arts and crafts. Maize, or corn, was the great discovery upon which their civilization was founded. No one knows when this plant was first domesticated, or exactly where, though there is reason to believe that it came from the highlands of Central America, the home of the early Mayas. Corn made it possible for the Mayas to build their sacred cities, where priest-rulers kept astronomical records and made the calendar upon which the corn-planting rituals were based.

The surprising definiteness of the dates given above is due to this calendar and to the Mayan custom of setting up stone markers, called "stelae," each year. These markers were dated to the very day they commemorated, and they were set up for some fifteen hundred years, a period of time longer than the entire Western culture of which we ourselves are a part.

THE MAYAN CALENDAR. The Mayan calendar year consisted of eighteen months of twenty days each, making three hundred and sixty days, plus four extra year-end days, and a "leap year" correction to take care of the few additional hours in the sun year. By this calendar, any day in a thirty-thousand-year interval could be named. Untold generations of priests must have studied the stars to have made this calendar, for even if some genius had invented the idea, he would have had to base it upon star records going back many years and upon a system of picture writing which must have taken centuries to develop. In addition to this sun calendar, the Mayas observed the changes of the planet Venus and made a Venus calendar.

Mayan thinkers, speculating about the beginning of the world, set the creation date at 3300 B.C., which is surprisingly close to the time set by our Church Fathers who, several centuries ago, announced that the world had been created in 4004 B.C. Both were slightly underestimating, according to modern scientists who believe our earth to be almost three billion years old, its probable age having been extended a billion years quite recently, to the consternation of astronomers who had figured the universe itself to be only two billion years old.

Mayan calendar dates and other records were written by means of symbols called "glyphs." The calendar glyphs—usually pictures of animals or gods—were luckily translated by Spanish priests shortly after the Conquest, but the calendar glyphs are the only Mayan pictographs which can at present be understood. To write a date, the Mayan artist drew an introducing glyph, then a second glyph showing which group of four thousand years the date fell in, then another glyph showing which twenty-year period, then a fourth naming the year itself, a fifth for the month, a sixth for the day, and then some following glyphs which made the whole thing clear, providing you were a Mayan priest. It is as if we wrote that Columbus discovered America in 1000, 400, 90, 2, 10, 12—with each number represented by a picture of a god or an animal.

THE NUMBER SYSTEM. Luckily, Mayan architects did not have to order their stone blocks in any such fashion, but made their calculations by means of a system something like a cross between Roman numerals and the Morse code. Figures one to four were dots, five was a bar, six to nine were a bar plus dots, etc., as follows:

MAYAN	ROMAN	MAYAN	ROMAN
.	I	—	V
..	II	·—	VI
...	III	··—	VII
....	IV	···—	VIII

In addition to having figured out this simple number system, the Mayan priests had invented the idea of zero, in which they were far ahead of our own ancestors, who never invented the zero at all but borrowed it from the Arabs after the Crusades.

MAYAN WRITING. The Mayas wrote by means of pictographs representing both sounds and ideas, somewhat as if you wrote "I saw a bee" by drawing an eye, a wood saw, and a bee. Once the meaning of such pictures is lost, the writing becomes a code almost impossible to break, because after centuries of use the pictures no longer look like the things they represented. The meaning of Chinese pictographs has been kept alive because the Chinese culture has been continuous. Egyptian hieroglyphs fell into disuse, but their meaning was luckily preserved by the famous Rosetta Stone, found by one of Napoleon's officers in Egypt, which showed a given inscription in two known languages and in hieroglyphs. Scholars seeking to decipher Mayan hieroglyphs have had no such luck and probably never will have. When the last Mayan priest died in about 1626, the secret of Mayan pictographs was lost. If some genius could figure out this forgotten writing, we might learn more of the history of the Mayas.

THE OLD MAYAN ERA. On the basis of the calendar and of weather lore preserved in their writings, Mayan priests were able to make predictions which made their power seem divine to the common people who tended the cornfields that stretched out into the countryside beyond the splendid cities which, from the fourth to the sixth centuries A.D., flourished in Guatemala and Honduras. The great city of Copán, in Honduras, was a sacred center at this

MAYAN ART

Left and right, characteristic designs on painted Mayan pottery; left center, painted vase; right center, polychrome vase

time. So were the twin cities of Uaxactun and Tikal, whose fantastic temples and marvelous works of art were only a part of a civilization which extended over a wide area during this "golden age" of the Mayas. Once our eyes have become accustomed to the strange style of this amazing art, so unlike that of our own traditions, we see why it takes its place with the best that man has ever produced.

Needless to say, this art development came after a long period of skill in handicrafts. Mayan pottery traveled far and wide, its broken shards remaining to help archaeologists trace out Mayan trade and travel routes. Examples of the potter's art show molded forms, human and animal, and abstract designs that compare well with the ceramics of any race. Mayan textiles were triumphs of weaving, dyeing, and embroidery, showing almost every known method of weaving and dyeing.

MAYAN TEMPLES. Mayan temples, towering into the air upon tall pyramidal bases, were monuments to the gods as well as stage settings for religious ceremonies, rather than meeting houses as our churches are. Small temples at their tops contained altar rooms or shrines in which the priests made prayers and sacrifices. The wide staircases leading up the pyramids were used for ceremonies. Priests in painted masks and colored plumes, in the flare of torches and the smoke of incense, must have looked like the gods themselves to worshipers gathered on the plaza below the pyramid.

Some ancient Mayan temples were astronomical observatories which also formed giant sundials. Several temples would be so designed that when certain planets rose directly behind them, as viewed perhaps from a passage location in a third temple, priests knew that the planting season had come.

Even the oldest known Mayan temples were built with an amazing architectural skill. Temples and palaces were often grouped around a large plaza, although in hilly regions architects used natural ridges as the bases for pyramids, and so a more informal grouping resulted. In the city of Copán, temples and palaces were grouped in a river valley, making a public center about eight hundred feet square. There a great amphitheater of cut stone was surrounded by tiers of seats rising one hundred and twenty feet. The inner walls of the buildings were painted, while outer walls were elaborately carved. It is remarkable that all these structures were built without the use of metal tools or beasts of burden.

Mayan architecture changed very slowly from century to century. Early temples were little more than altars built on top of pyramids. Later pyramids were topped by small temples with rooms inside them.

A Mayan pyramid, unlike an Egyptian one, was cut off at the top, which thus became the base for the temple. The Mayas were constantly rebuilding their public buildings. Older ones were often covered with earth to form a new pyramid. This makes a difficult problem for archaeologists, who have to excavate the older buried temple without letting the later pyramid and temple collapse. After the earth was shaped into a pyramid, Mayan builders put forms against it and filled them in with stones, rubble, and mortar, which hardened into a mixture like concrete. The sloping sides of the pyramid were finished with a layer of stucco or perhaps faced with carved stone blocks.

THE MAYAN DARK AGES. The seventh century A.D. was a period of decline for the Mayas as well as for Europeans. For two centuries they went through what we would call a depression. Construction of great public buildings stopped. Many cities were abandoned altogether.

Archaeologists have tried in every possible way to find out what destroyed the Mayan civilization of the first era. Was it civil war? Invasion? Natural disasters such as volcanic eruptions, rising mountains, and long droughts have also been suggested as explanations, but such events would have left unmistakable traces.

Many such theories to account for the abandonment of Mayan cities have been put forth, but the Mayan authority, Dr. Sylvanus Morley, has concluded that the chief explanation of Mayan Dark Age migrations is that their corn-planting system broke down. With new jungles to be burned over and planted to corn, the Mayan system could flourish. But after the forests were destroyed, the stubborn roots of grass crept in like a strangling web and choked out the corn. Grass roots could not be burned away, and a pointed digging stick was no defense against such an enemy.

When the cornfields no longer produced enough food for the

population, the city dwellers had either to leave their homes or trade craft products for food. If the same thing happened over a wide area, the Mayas would have had to move away to some place where there were fresh jungles to burn over. People from the depressed cities must have tried desperately to find new regions in which to begin again. Some of them may have gone by boat across the Gulf of Mexico, perhaps as explorer parties in search of sites for colonization. As we saw in our study of the Mound Builders of the Mississippi and Ohio river valleys, there are very strong evidences of considerable Mexica-Mayan art influence in this region. It is possible that small Mayan colonies attempted to found a new Mayan culture here, but were too few in number and were absorbed by the native population. Or perhaps the explanation is that during this period of wandering, small Mayan explorer parties carried Mayan ideas and symbols to what is now the United States area, where they later became meaningless signs carved on shell gorgets, and confused legends about birdmen and serpent-bird gods.

Other wanderers may have gone in increasing numbers southward, looking for jungles to burn over and limestone to use in softening corn kernels and in binding mortar for temple building. Mayan colonization efforts remind us of the Biblical parable of the seeds that could not grow because they fell on stony ground or among weeds. Of the Mayan cultural seeds, only those that fell upon limestone were able to take root and to blossom into a reborn Mayan culture. Perhaps our own southern Gulf area failed to provide exactly the right combination of conditions for the transplanting of this culture.

THE NEW MAYAN ERA. In the arid peninsula of Yucatán, however, Mayan wanderers managed to grow corn in such abundance that again the great white temples and palaces of the priests and nobles rose. If the settlers missed the beauty of their highland country, there was all the more reason for building tall pyramids.

In Yucatán the Mayas found no rivers and few lakes, but at places where the limestone floor of the peninsula had caved in, they found deep sinkholes filled with water. Around the largest of these *cenotes*, cities grew up in which, by 999 A.D., when the Christians of Europe were quaking in their boots, knowing very well that they were not ready for the second coming of Christ which was expected in 1000 A.D., the Mayas were enjoying a renaissance of arts and crafts in Yucatán. For two centuries their artists and architects created temples and other art works that would have been a credit to any race.

MAYAN SCULPTURE AND PAINTING. The Mayan artists of Yucatán who modeled and painted temple walls and carved designs on stone building blocks were extremely skillful. Mayan boys who showed a talent for art must have undergone a long training period. They did not draw directly from life but copied forms used by their ancestors. This way of drawing, as we have seen, is called conventional because it follows fixed rules or conventions. Drawing in this way, they produced art so removed from life that it is now hard to know exactly what the designs were meant to portray. An example of this difficulty is found in the popular symbol of the plumed serpent, which is often so conventionalized that it is hard to recognize. The plaster figures from the wall of the Temple of the Chacmool, Chichen Itzá, were made in a late period, after naturalistic art had reached Yucatán from Mexico.

Mayan painting has been largely destroyed by the damp, de-vouring jungle, while wind, rain, and sun have stripped the color from the carved temple walls. But fortunately a few inside walls fell down in such a way that rain and sun could not get at the paintings which adorned them.

Ann Axtell Morris, working with her archaeologist husband, Earl Morris, at the tremendous job of restoring Chichen Itzá, patiently fitted together hundreds of scattered bits of stone and stucco to restore paintings that time had destroyed. One such, from the Temple of the Warriors, is a seascape in which strange creatures of sea and land, houses, trees, boats, and people are all jumbled together in a lively way. Another fresco from the same temple shows warriors conquering a city. Protected by helmets, padded armor, and shields, they scramble into undersized houses and temples. Priests in ceremonial black lead captives off to the sacrifice. Another fresco from this same temple shows a woodland scene which might be a Mayan Garden of Eden.

Woodworking was also a Mayan specialty, and the making of wooden idols was a very serious business for Mayan artists. Idols were carved from cedar wood, then sprinkled with blood and scented with copal, a kind of resin from certain tropical trees, used by the Indians for incense. This work took place in a certain month, after due fasting and prayer, in a special house which was closely guarded. Despite these precautions, the idol makers believed that their craft was dangerous and that one of their number would die or fall ill, a sacrifice to the gods.

RECORDS LEFT BY THE MAYAS. Our discussion of the Old Mayan era had to be based on the research of archaeologists working at the sites of the forgotten Mayan cities, and thus dealt with architecture and art, the only surviving relics of the culture. But our study of the new Mayas of Yucatán is enriched by records left by late Mayan priests and their Spanish conquerors. These Mayan records are few, due to the misplaced zeal of a Spanish bishop named Landa, who went to Yucatán in 1548 as a young monk. Considering the Mayan books the work of the devil, Landa gathered them together and set fire to them. "As the sacred Maya records burst into flames," he later wrote, "the Maya priests broke into a wail of despair." Anthropologists echo this wail. The soul of Mayan civilization went up in smoke that day, when the astronomical records, the ancient history, the religious ritual, and the accumulated wisdom and knowledge of two thousand years were destroyed.

Though Landa was extraordinarily successful in his aim to destroy the Mayan culture, the records of three families of priest-nobles, written after the Conquest, in Latin characters, escaped him. The story of the Tutul-Xiu, a ruling family of Chichen Itzá, is told in the *Books of Chilam Balam*, the "Tiger Priest." The *Popul Vuh* contains the sacred history of the Quiché tribe of Guatemala; and the *Annals*, that of the Xahila family of the same region. Partly to justify himself for having destroyed the Mayan records, Bishop Landa wrote about Mayan customs in his "Account of Things of Yucatán." This *Relación de las Cosas de Yucatán* lay forgotten in the Royal Academy of History in Madrid, but when it was discovered, the students of Mayan history learned from it how to read the dates on some of the Mayan monuments.

With these records, and the patient toil of archaeologists, as a basis of knowledge, let us exercise our imagination to visit the new Mayan city of Chichen Itzá, in whose streets and temples you may some day actually wander. Let us drop back almost a thousand years. Our Saxon and Norman ancestors were settling down together in England, and at Chichen Itzá the refugees from the Old Mayan cities had in the same way blended with Toltec strains, to build pyramids and temples at this site, the name of which means "Mouth of the Well of the Itzás." We will visit this city as it might have been seen by a boy of the Itzá nobility, free for a day from his task of learning the sciences of priesthood. We will call him Nohkukum, an old Mayan name which means "Big Feather." Let us imagine that this story takes place at about the time that William the Conqueror and his Norman barons were engaged in the conquest of England, in 1066. Though our story is imaginary, it is based on knowledge assiduously built up by many archaeologists.

A DAY IN CHICHEN ITZÁ. Though it was still dark when Nohkukum woke, he heard the cheerful voices of kitchen women already at work over their grinding stones. The "chush, chush"

from the grinding stones was followed by "pat, pat, pat" as the
women's quick hands slapped dough into flat pancakes to be baked
over the fire.

Suddenly remembering that this was a very important day,
Nohkukum jumped from his bed, tied a loincloth about his waist,
stepped into his deerskin sandals, and ran to the grass-thatched
kitchen hut. Here he found the women bustling about as they
prepared many exciting foods. Peeking into the various pots,
Nohkukum saw black beans seasoned with pepper, a cut of deer,
a haunch of wild hog, and other appetizing things to eat.

A country boy his own age was unloading fish, turtle eggs, and
fresh game under the eye of the steward, who made an account
of all foodstuffs as they were brought in. The boys looked at each

other but did not speak. Nohkukum's father was an important official whose household was kept supplied with food by workers from the many little thatched huts crowded together beyond the handsome stone-faced houses belonging to the nobility.

When Nohkukum was younger, he had wished he could trade places with these farmer boys who hunted and fished without ever having to bother with the study of astronomical and religious lore. Even now, at the time of the burning of the brush from the cornfields, when at night the great bonfires lit the sky, Nohkukum sometimes envied them. Now no one had to remind him, however, that men of his family were rulers whose work was different and far greater. One of his uncles was a judge famous for settling disputes and for improving the efficient Mayan law-court system. Another was an architect who designed and built the great new temples and monuments. A third was the engineer who planned and laid out the roads that led from Chichen Itzá to many other Mayan cities.

As Nohkukum ate his breakfast he watched the goings-on in the kitchen court. Today was a very special day. No one had to leave for the daily work in the cornfields and salt mines or on the roads or public buildings. Everyone in Chichen Itzá would be at the Sacred Well, taking part in the ceremonies to the Rain God, who seemed to have turned his back on suffering humankind.

Nohkukum scooped up a last mouthful of beans with his corncake. Then he rinsed his mouth and fingers in the bowl a servant woman handed him. Soon after leaving his own house, he passed a temple which was being rebuilt under his uncle's direction. Knowing that work would be suspended today, on an impulse Nohkukum ran up the tall flight of stairs. Up and up and up he toiled, now and then pausing to catch his breath. At last he reached the top. Surely no one had ever before honored a god with such a tall pyramid as this one! Here on top was the temple of the god: a rectangular building which Nohkukum did not dare

enter, even now. Below him, the pyramid dropped down in nine great terraces, each steep wall decorated with carved stone. The streets were such a dizzy depth below him that people looked no larger than his sister's toys. From here he could look down upon all of Chichen Itzá. Its white pyramids of different heights and shapes gleamed in the rising sun. Many were completely constructed of fancifully carved stones. One was surrounded with hundreds of stone columns. On and on Chichen Itzá extended in its dazzling beauty—and so it would stand forever, thought Nohkukum, as he made his way down the long stairway toward the crowded plaza.

It would be wonderful to be an architect like his uncle, he thought. But Nohkukum knew there were many things an architect must learn. His uncle spent countless days making plans and drawings to show how his buildings were to look, and adding long rows of figures to estimate how many and what size building stones and wooden beams would be needed. For hours on end he argued with older priests, who doggedly defended ancient ways of building and would not try newer ones. Months and even years went into the construction itself.

As Nohkukum passed a great ball court located between two temples, he paused to look inside. For once there were no *pok'- ta-pok* players at practice. Here the smooth plaster walls were adorned with paintings of gods. In the center of the two end walls were carved stone rings opposite each other. Nohkukum had often watched players struggle wildly to put a ball through the opponent's ring, hitting it with head, shoulders, arms, or hips, but never with hands or feet. Only once had he been present when a certain player, by a skillful twist of the hips, had bounced the heavy ball of native jungle rubber through the ring. There had been a moment's stunned silence among the crowd, followed by wild cheering. Then everyone had made a mad rush away from the ball court, since the player who put the ball through the ring was by custom entitled to as much of the jewelry and clothing of the spectators as his friends could snatch from those unlucky enough to be caught.

Though it was still early, the streets of Chichen Itzá were already crowded. All night a continual stream of people had poured into the sacred city from countryside and villages. Shaggy-haired farmers, burned three shades darker than the city folk, held hands with their wives and children. Fishermen from coastal regions, still smelling of fish, stared with open mouths at the towering pyramids. Richly dressed merchants, their ears and lower lips handsomely set with gold plugs, were followed by

slaves carrying bundles on their backs: the bundles were supported by head straps around their foreheads. Nohkukum could imagine what would be in them: copper bells, golden dishes and ornaments from Mexico, black obsidian knives and jewelry from the volcanic mountains, and bright feathers from tropical regions.

Here came a group of warriors, roughly pushing people aside with their shields. Nohkukum thought they looked splendid in their towering helmets, but he guessed that they were much too warm in their cotton-padded armor. Town officials scurried past with worried frowns. A great noble passed in a litter carried by slaves, his pet dog running underneath. The nobleman's brilliant feather headdress glittered. His teeth were splendidly set with turquoise and his eyes were handsomely crossed—an effect achieved by a doting mother who had hung a dangling object in front of her baby's eyes in order to make him conform to Mayan beauty standards.

Through a temple doorway Nohkukum caught sight of black-painted priests preparing for the sacrifice ritual. They were tense and strained, with the same expression of fear and worry on every face. Nohkukum knew that times were very bad. For many months it had not rained, and crops were parching in the sun. If rain did not come soon, there would be no corn to eat this year. Nor was this all. There were rumors that an enemy army was gathering in cities farther north. Trade was at a standstill. Even the public works planned to keep people busy could not employ all the idle men.

Today the desperate priests were to make the final sacrifice to the gods. Often before, they had thrown rich offerings of jewelry and other precious objects into the Sacred Well. But on this anxious day they were to make the most precious sacrifice of all: the beautiful daughter of one of the high priests. Would she live, to return to them with good news from the Rain God's abode? The chance was slight; still, it had sometimes happened so.

Nohkukum joined the procession winding toward the Sacred *Cenote* where the sacrifice was to take place. Solemn people, following one another in a long line, stopped at a little altar to make their prayers. This done, they filed one by one past the edge of the Sacred Well which yawned before them a hundred and fifty feet wide. No one could look down into the great *cenote* without fear. Its dark walls went down, down, into the black water far below.

Into this fearful well people now were flinging offerings: golden bells, beads carved from jade, rings and ornaments of copper, sandals, idols of wood or stone, and balls of sweet-burning copal.

The merchant ahead of Nohkukum had on his face a look of fear and cunning as he threw a white ball of copal into the sacred waters. Nohkukum could not know that the man was wondering if the gods would know that this ball was not copal all the way through but had a center of grass, as the archaeologists who dredged it from the well centuries later were to discover.

There was a hush. Silence fell over the crowd as a gorgeous procession advanced slowly. All eyes turned to the two priests, wearing jaguar skins and sacred masks glittering with metal and feather ornaments, who led between them a lovely girl wreathed in clouds of incense. Dazed by drugs given her, the girl made no sound but walked as if in sleep as she was led to the edge of the Sacred Well. Priests chanted the prayer that the sacrifice might be accepted, that the gods would relent, be merciful, and send rains. But when the two priests holding the girl's arms swung her out into the air and she disappeared into the depths below, the watchers suddenly heard her last, despairing cry. Then a wail went up from the crowd.

*   *   *

For hundreds of years after this imaginary scene is supposed to have taken place, the treasures and the bones of people who had actually been sacrificed in some such way lay undisturbed in the mud of the great *cenote* at Chichen Itzá. Then, over four hundred years after the discovery of America, archaeologists began to investigate the mounds of earth that covered the site of the ancient Mayan city. Fired by stories told by the natives of the region, an American who was interested in the ancient history of Yucatán decided to dredge the *cenote*.

At first, there seemed to be nothing there at all but the deposit of centuries of humdrum processes of nature, which had built thick layers of mud and decayed leaves. The searchers began to fear that the old legends were nothing more than invented stories. Then, just as they were about to give up in disappointment, there in the mud someone saw two little white balls. Cleaned and cut open, they were found to be made of the resin copal. Then hundreds of other objects were found: golden basins and cups, dozens of dishes of beaten gold, rings, masks, shields, beads of jade and bells of gold, pottery, crowns, cloth, spearheads, and the other treasures that the people of Chichen Itzá had offered to the gods.

With these objects there were the bones of human beings—not many, but enough to make it seem likely that there was truth in the old legends that told of human sacrifices in the Sacred *Cenote*.

MAYAN GODS. Thanks to Bishop Landa and to the Mayan records, we know that the late Mayas worshiped a variety of gods, with at least twelve major gods and a number of minor ones, some good, some bad. Their chief god, Kukulcan, was none other than the great Plumed Serpent god known in Mexico as Quetzalcoatl, the wind god whose feathers symbolized the ripple of wind on water, the breath of life itself, the union of sky and earth. Kukulcan, according to the usual legend, had been the "Fair God" who taught his people writing. A round structure at Chichen Itzá, the Caracol, may have been dedicated to this god, and at the same time designed to serve a practical purpose as an astronomical observatory. The temple called "El Castillo," also associated with the wind god, is constructed with eighteen terraces for the eighteen months in the Mayan calendar, and three hundred and sixty steps for the days in the year.

The four and a fraction of extra days of the sun year were not a part of the calendar year, and so were not numbered in the steps of the Temple of Kukulcan, but they were a period of great stress in the lives of the Mayas. On the last day of the old year, householders cleaned house and renewed household objects, while priests fasted and prayed that the gods would grant them another year. The new year opened on one of the four extra days, which were presided over by four gods called "year bearers," who also were thought to hold in place the four corners of the earth. Everyone rejoiced when the cycle of days fixed the beginning of the year on the day of the god of the South, whose color was yellow, or the god of the East, whose color was red, because these were reasonable gods who might bring in a good year. The god of the North, whose color was white, was less pleasant, but times were really critical when the god of the West, whose color was black, was the year bearer. This god brought death and destruction, to avoid which the Mayas redoubled their offerings, sacrifices, and the rites such as dancing on burning coals, when it was his time to bring in the new year.

There were, in addition, the agricultural gods and goddesses, the weather gods, and those who looked after the people of certain professions. There was even a god of beekeepers!

MAYAN PRIESTS. The rituals by which the gods were served were performed by an aristocracy of priest-nobles whose great power

often passed from father to son. These high priests elected and trained the young people who were to become priests. They rarely appeared before the people except during the awe-inspiring religious ceremonies. They spoke for the gods and expected to become gods themselves after death.

They alone knew how to read the calendar and thus when to plant crops. Weather lore centuries old helped them to foretell rains and other seasonal changes, eclipses, comets, and such natural phenomena. Since the common people did not know that the priests learned these things from their carefully guarded secret records, they thought the priests had power over the sun, moon, and stars. We can understand why the priests wailed when the Spaniards burned the Mayan records: they knew their magic-making powers, along with the history of their race, were gone forever. Below the high priests, trained in predicting eclipses and other astronomical events, were lesser priests who carried on sacrifices, and presided over prayers made to the gods of war, earth, hunting, agriculture, rain, birth, and death.

The Mayan gods, according to legend, had made several attempts to create men from clay, wood, and straw. When these men had proved too stupid to worship their creators properly, the gods destroyed them by means of a flood; a few escaped to the trees and so became monkeys. Then man was created from cornmeal and blood, and the gods settled back to be worshiped. The Mayas tried hard to keep their gods satisfied, and either looked forward to going to a heaven where nobody had to raise corn, or feared going to an ice-cold Hell.

Mayan religious rites do not seem to have included much human sacrifice. Recent studies by Dr. Hooton of Harvard show that only forty-two individuals can be reassembled from the bones in the Sacred *Cenote* at Chichen Itzá. Some were doubtless children who fell in; battered-looking adults may have been pushed in for personal reasons.

THE DECLINE OF THE MAYAN CIVILIZATION. In 1000 A.D., Chichen Itzá, the best known of the New Mayan cities in Yucatán, joined with two rival cities, Uxmal and Mayapán, to form a confederacy, the League of Mayapán. This league kept some measure of peace for two centuries, but by the twelfth century civil war had developed. There is a romantic legend that the rulers of the city-states quarreled over some Mayan Helen of Troy, who may have been especially endowed with the usual Mayan beauty marks of inlaid teeth, deformed forehead, and tattooed cheeks. Economic causes, such as a struggle for food supplies, are a more likely explanation.

Whatever the true cause, the Mayan city-states in Yucatán went to war and were never at peace again. Now one city, then another, hired mercenaries from Mexico to come and fight for them, which caused further trouble. In 1194 Uxmal and Chichen Itzá were captured and their rulers brought to Mayapán, which then ruled Yucatán for some two centuries. But revolt simmered in the conquered cities and in 1441 broke loose again.

In 1450 Chichen Itzá was sacked and came at last to the end of its thousand-year history as a center of Mayan religious life. It had been as important to generations of people as Mecca is to the Moslems or as Jerusalem was to the Crusaders. Under the stress of civil war, however, the survivors forgot the learning and arts of their ancestors.

The white man is not to blame for the destruction of Mayan civilization. The real trouble was probably that the corn-growing system, which depended on burning over new jungles, had again broken down. The magic of Mayan priests could not work against such enemies as civil war, the wearing out of the soil, the disappearance of the jungle, long periods of drought, or the relentless growth of grass. Then, too, the Mayan civilization rested on a form of slavery in which many humble people supported a small ruling class of priests and nobles. Such a system depends on the public virtues of the rulers. In the late Mayan era the rulers were probably arrogant Mexica-Mayans who kept their power not by skill and wisdom in caring for their people but by means of hired mercenary soldiers. This was government without the "consent of the governed."

THE SPANISH CONQUEST. Like the city-states of the Greeks, those of the Mayas could not defend themselves from foreign invaders after they had become weakened by civil wars. During the Spanish Conquest, the Xiu, the rulers of Chichen Itzá, actually helped the conquerors instead of standing with other Mayas against the common enemy.

A few of the Mayas escaped southward to an island in Lake Petén, where they were able to resist the Spaniards until 1697. Others retreated to the wooded coastlands of the west, where their descendants were only recently conquered by Mexico's President

Díaz. Though three hundred thousand people still speak the Mayan tongues, none of them can read the records left by their ancestors. The great Mayan civilization disappeared when the only educated people, the priest-nobles, were destroyed.

And so there came to an end the story of a people who for two thousand years had created impressive art and architecture, who had been broken first by famine, disease, and civil wars, and who were given a final blow by the Spanish conquerors, with their book burnings, tortures, killings, and mass slavery.

But the conquerors found little of interest in the civilization of the Mayas, which had produced beautiful temples in stone but few treasures in gold. So the Spaniards, too, abandoned the Mayan cities. The jungle crept back over the grass-choked cornfields and up the sides of the mounds where the beautiful stone temples had stood. In the grass-roofed huts the descendants of the Mayas lived simple lives, the arts and skills of their ancestors forgotten.

FROM A MAYAN LAMENT AGAINST THE SPANISH CONQUERORS

Then began the building of the church
Here in the center of Tihoo:
Great labor is the destiny of the katun.
Then began the execution by hanging,
And the fire at the ends of their hands.
Then also came ropes and cords into the world.
Then came the children of the younger brothers
Under the hardship of legal summons and tribute.
Tribute was introduced on a large scale,
And Christianity was introduced on a large scale.
Then the seven sacraments of God's word were established.
Receive your guests heartily; our elder brothers come!

XI. THE MEXICAN
MELTING POT

A Song by Nezahualcoyotl

(AZTEC)

The sweet-voiced *quetzal* there, ruling the earth, has intoxicated my soul.

I am like the quetzal bird, I am created in the one and only God; I sing sweet songs among the flowers; I chant songs and rejoice in my heart.

The fuming dewdrops from the flowers in the fields intoxicate my soul.

I grieve to myself that ever this dwelling on earth should end.

I foresaw, being a Mexican, that our rule began to be destroyed, I went forth weeping that it was to bow down and to be destroyed.

Let me not be angry that the grandeur of Mexico is to be destroyed.

The smoking stars gather against it; the one who cares for flowers is about to be destroyed.

He who cared for books wept, he wept for the beginning of the destruction.

This lovely poem by a Mexican priest-ruler perfectly expresses the Mexican love of flowers and life, and the sense of life's tragic brevity, in terms which remind us of the Hebrew psalmist's words. The sense of a coming doom was very strong among the Mexica-Mayan Indians just before the Conquest. The "smoking stars" was a comet which appeared to be taken as an omen of destruction.

THE MEXICAN MELTING POT

WHEN we look at America as time carved it rather than as man has divided it, we see that the great highway down the Central Plains extends southward into Mexico. Near the area occupied for some two thousand years by the Basketmaker Pueblos, the plateau dips to form the valley through which the Rio Grande flows into the Gulf of Mexico. Beyond this valley the plateau rises again and sweeps grandly down the length of Mexico. A thousand miles south of the Rio Grande is a high and beautiful valley ringed with volcanoes: the valley of Mexico.

Ages ago there was a great shallow lake in this high valley. As the early hunters followed the game herds down the Americas, some of them settled around the shores of this lake. Thousands of years later, when Columbus discovered America, he might have discovered a great city built in the shallow remnant of this lake. This was Tenochtitlán, the capital city of the Mexicas, who are usually called the Aztecs.

ANCIENT MAN DISCOVERS MEXICO. The country of which Tenochtitlán was a part had a long history behind it, as the archaeologists have discovered. Many different people lived in Mexico before the Aztecs built that great and beautiful city. For the Aztecs or Mexicas were late-comers to the valley of Mexico. Back in the days of Sandia and Folsom men, bands of hunters passed down the great plateau into Mexico. They traveled down to the warm seashore to escape winter's cold or climbed to the high plateau to escape summer's heat. Basketmaking seed gatherers searched out the natural food crops, discovering a seed grass which became maize or "teocentli," the Aztec "food of the gods." Centuries went into the improvement of corn as a food plant, and meanwhile people domesticated other plants, learned to spin and weave and to make pots and dishes. This "archaic" or old-fashioned corn-planting culture was widely spread over Central America before the time of Christ. The early people of the valley of Mexico made good pottery, modeled small female idols, spun and wove, used tools of bone, obsidian, and quartz, and built adobe houses. Later, they traded with more distant tribes, bringing in shells, ornaments, jade, and pottery made in other regions.

THE TOLTECS BUILD GREAT RELIGIOUS CENTERS. By the eighth century traders had made contact with the Mayan cities in Central America, returning with ornaments of jade, mother-of-pearl, mosaics, metalwork and the brightly colored feathers of the quetzal bird. The ancient people who built their towns around the lake in the valley of Mexico were known to the Aztecs, who came later, as "Toltecs," or "Skilled Workers."

The Toltec communities became religious centers where great temples were built on tall pyramids. It is likely that some sort of political or religious federation banded the settlements loosely together. The Toltec city of San Juan Teotihuacán, where you can climb a pyramid that still towers one hundred and eighty feet into the air, may have been a religious center. Near this great Pyramid of the Sun are lesser temples, all of which were covered with earth some centuries before the white men discovered America.

Fifty miles north of the modern capital of Mexico was another ancient city, Tula or Tullan, which may have been the seat of government of these ancient people. Objects from Tula are found as far away as Copán in Honduras. A third great center of pre-Aztec times was at Cholula, where what looks like a natural mountain was discovered to be another enormous pyramid, the largest known. This one is a thousand feet on each side at the base and covers twice as much ground space as does the Egyptian pyramid of Cheops. Cholula was occupied by many different people as the years passed. When the Spanish arrived, they found so many temples that when they had massacred the population and set out to build churches where the temples had been, they had to build so many that Cholula now boasts of having "a church for every day in the year."

The Toltec people learned a great deal from the early Mayas, whose cities in Honduras and southern Mexico were declining at about this time. Perhaps wanderers from the Mayan cities went northward to Mexico, or perhaps Toltec trading expeditions went to the Mayan centers, as they did in later Aztec days. They probably returned with jade, gold, cacao, jaguar skins, and other treasures, for which they may have traded pottery and feather-work from Cholula, woven baskets and decorated gourds from Texcoco, pottery from Puebla, and paints, dyes, obsidian knives, and copper bells from Tenochtitlán. Many things besides objects of art came north from the Maya region. The calendar, we are told, used day signs represented by animals unknown in Mexico but familiar in the Mayan jungles. Quetzalcoatl, the Plumed Serpent god, was known to both peoples.

MEXICAN ART

Left: Incensario of the Teoti-huacán culture of the Valley of Mexico; upper right: Effigy vase found with a burial of the Mazapan culture at Teoti-huacán; lower right: Clay mask found at Vera Cruz; center: Mexican pottery jars

THE AZTECS ARRIVE IN MEXICO. Centuries of easy living, of religious rituals, arts, and crafts made the Toltec people an easy prey to barbaric nomadic tribes who swept down on them from the north. About 1325 A.D. one such tribe, the Aztecs, who had

left a northern home called Aztlán, built the lake city of Tenochtitlán, where Mexico City now stands. Aztlán is now thought to
have been in North America, since the Aztec language is like that
used among certain North American tribes.

The Aztecs or, as anthropologists prefer to call them, the
Mexicas may have settled here and there for various lengths of
time during the hundreds of years after they had left their un-
identified home. Perhaps they had fought their way down the
west coast of Mexico before they settled at last on pile buildings
in the waters of Lake Texcoco.

Although already in decline, the Toltecs were still powerful
enough to prevent the Mexicas from settling on the good land
beside the lake. They mockingly told the strangers that they could
live among the reeds in the mud flats, thinking that no one could
live in such a place. But the Mexicas were hard to discourage.
They built rafts, or islands of reeds and twigs, upon which they
spread mud dredged from the lake bottom, and so provided themselves with gardens in which to grow their food. Flimsy huts were
built on these contrived islands, and a variety of plants were cultivated which eventually thrust their way through the woven floor
and took root in the bottom of the lake. Even today, thousands of
admiring tourists can see the remains of what became a flourishing island empire, in the famous Floating Gardens of Xochimilco,
southwest of Mexico City.

By 1380 the Mexicas had won from the Tepanec tribe of the
Toltec people the right to pipe water from the spring of Chapul-
tepec. Under Itzcouatl, who ruled from 1427 to 1440, the Aztecs
overthrew the Tepanec and made a league with the people of
Texcoco and Tlacopa. Later they conquered all the valley of
Mexico and reached the frontiers of modern Guatemala.

LIFE IN TENOCHTITLÁN IN THE TIME OF MONTEZUMA. Tenochtitlán, as Spanish conquerors were to find it in 1519, was a magnificent city. Its great temples and enormous palaces were set on

man-made islands among green and flowering gardens watered by canals. The dazzled Spaniards said, "It is like the enchantments they tell of in the Legend of Amadis. Are not the things we see a dream?"

Montezuma, the last Aztec war chief, was a ruler so powerful that only a few people ever dared look at him; he ruled over much of what is now Mexico.

Let us visit his capital, Tenochtitlán, as it might have been seen through the eyes of a boy of the Mexica tribe. It is the day after the Spaniards landed at Vera Cruz, a spot on the eastern seacoast, in 1519. Our guide is named Ocelotl, a good Aztec name that means "ocelot," or Mexican tiger. He is a farmer boy who lives on the outskirts of Tenochtitlán in the district which even today is called Xochimilco, or "Blooming Field." Here gardens surrounded by canals supplied the Aztec capital with food and flowers, just as today they supply Mexico City, which rises above the ruins of Tenochtitlán.

A DAY IN TENOCHTITLÁN. Ocelotl knew that he ought to be sorry that his father had hurt his foot, but he could not help feeling elated because he was going to the market all by himself. His dugout canoe was piled high with corn, peppers, squash, and other vegetables and bright fruits. It was a beautiful clear day. Above the treetops the snow-covered volcanoes, Popocatepetl, the Smoking One, and Iztaccihuatl, the Sleeping One, shone like white clouds against the blue sky. The *centzentli*, the "bird of four hundred songs," sang from the tops of the willow trees that lined the canal and towered high above mud-and-wattle walls and thatched roofs where farmer families lived.

Ocelotl poled his dugout along the canal. Idly he recalled how his grandmother had told him that in the days of her own grandfather there had been no gardens and canals here. There had been only a reedy island in a lake, beside which his weary ancestors paused after their long wandering. As they rested here, they saw an eagle gliding over the lake. Suddenly it swooped down upon a cactus growing on the island and from its branches pulled a large snake. With awe in their hearts, the wanderers remembered how the god Huitzilopochtli had long ago appeared in a vision to tell them: "Go until you find a place where an eagle on a cactus kills a serpent. Build your city there."

However, as Ocelotl's grandmother had told him, rich and powerful tribes had lived in the broad valley that surrounded the lake. They were town-dwelling people who had built enormous temples to the sun—pyramids that seemed to challenge the two volcanoes that towered over the valley. These people denied land to the weary Mexicas but permitted them to settle on the little island in the lake, thinking they would soon die of starvation. But the newcomers did not starve. Ocelotl's grandmother had been told by her own grandmother how the women had woven big rafts of roots and reeds, which men and boys had covered with mud scooped from the bottom of the lake. On these little islands they had planted vegetables and trees, whose roots in time had pushed down into the lake bed to form these island gardens.

Next the Mexicas had wanted to build a temple to their War God, Huitzilopochtli, the "Hummingbird of the South." This they could not do with twigs and mud. So they had traded with nearby tribes, exchanging fish, ducks, and frogs for wood, lime, and rock with which to build the temple. The Mexicas were crafty; they had paid tribute to the powerful tribes who could have destroyed them and had asked for women from these tribes, to become wives of their rulers. By such devices they became strong enough in time to conquer the tribes about them, one by one. In this way Tenochtitlán had become the great and splendid capital of an empire.

Now Ocelotl reached the main canal beside one of the four great causeways leading from the mainland to the two islands on which Tenochtitlán stood. Here were fine adobe houses that dazzled the eye with the white of plaster or the tawny color of powdered pumice. Though it was only a little after dawn, the wide causeway was already crowded with people. Ocelotl watched a merchant go past with his retinue of soldier guards, followed by carriers who trotted along, supporting packs on their backs with tumplines across their foreheads. Ocelotl wondered if they were going down to the hot country for jaguar skins, jade, and bright feathers, or up to the highlands for gold, copper, and obsidian.

By now the canal was thronged with canoes that were loaded with vegetables and flowers. Dodging in and out among traffic, Ocelotl at last reached the market place. His first concern was to locate his mother's sister, to whom he carried various messages. When he had found her at her usual place in the market, he knelt down beside her to arrange his own vegetables and flowers in neat piles on a woven mat. His aunt took charge of his produce, saying that, as likely as not, if he sold it, he would be swindled and would wind up the day without even his sandals. Ocelotl waited until she was busy with a customer, and then he slipped away into the crowd, knowing his aunt would have to stay where she was for some hours.

Tenochtitlán was too great a city for a small boy to explore in one morning, but Ocelotl did his best. At first it was fun merely to wander around looking at the people. The market was thronged with shoppers who pushed their way from one booth to another, talking, laughing, trading, thumping a fruit or fingering a beautifully woven cloth, shrugging their shoulders and walking away if the price seemed too high. Inspectors walked through the crowds to see that honest weights were given. Now and then they dragged a frightened cheater off to answer to the judges for his misconduct. Black-robed priests passed, their hair matted and their ear lobes showing dried blood where they had been pierced with thorns, in penitence for sins. Now and then the crowds parted to

give way to warriors, whose war clubs, toothed with sharp obsidian, commanded respect. In a cleared space a group of hunchbacked jugglers tossed their balls of jungle-made rubber. Musicians, carrying their drums and fifes, pushed their way toward a temple courtyard.

Then a group of poorly dressed people with wooden bars across their shoulders passed Ocelotl, and he was glad that none of his family had had to sell themselves into slavery. Remembering a friend of his father who had gambled away his own freedom at the ball game not long before, Ocelotl had a sudden desire to visit the ball court. On his way there he paused outside the stone gates of a nobleman's house. From within came the thin, piercing notes of flutes, the shrill piping of pottery whistles, the rattle of gourds filled with pebbles, and the shrieks of excited dancers. Ocelotl learned from the ancient doorman sitting at his post that a fiesta honoring the god "Two Rabbit" was in progress. The boy wrinkled his brown nose and sniffed the rich air that floated from the doorway. Above the cloying sweet of incense came a spicy smell of food that made his mouth water. A pungent whiff came from the corner where the men over fifty were enjoying the privilege of their age, that of getting drunk. Ocelotl wanted to stay, but the watchman eyed him suspiciously and he moved on toward the ball court.

At the ball court a practice game was in progress. Ocelotl picked one player as a favorite, but though the player sent the ball swiftly from one end of the court to another, skillfully hitting it with hips and knees, he could not put it through the stone ring set high in the wall. As Ocelotl knew, this was so difficult that, when it did happen, the player was entitled by ancient custom to whatever clothes and ornaments his friends could capture from the wildly scattering crowd.

Since Ocelotl had more curiosity than judgment, now and then in the next hour he poked his brown face into places where he had no business. However, those who noticed the farmer boy supposed that he was busy with some errand. Once Ocelotl found himself in a court where clan leaders were assembled. He saw an old man bending over maps. Before him stood two farmers, each claiming the right to a certain piece of land. Ocelotl knew the law: that if land was not tilled properly for three years, it must be taken away from the bad farmer. The lazy-looking, scowling man was defending himself from the charge of having neglected his fields, while the other claimed that he should be allowed to farm them, what with all the mouths he had to feed. Ocelotl had little sympathy for the lazy farmer; his own father worked hard to keep his land in good use.

Wandering on, Ocelotl found himself in a small plaza whence steps rose steeply up a tall pyramid. From one side of the plaza came the sound of boys' voices and the clash of weapons. Following the noise, he came upon a milling group of boys fighting with flat clubs and small wooden shields. One boy ducked a hard blow and started to turn away from his opponent, but at a sharp word from the scarred, hard-faced teacher, he began fighting again. There, also, a small group of boys were practicing the use of the *atlatl*, a grooved throwing stick grasped in the hand to hold the spear for careful balance, accurate aim, and lengthened flight. These boys, the sons of warriors, were in training to follow their fathers' profession. Their futures depended upon their skill at fighting, for the young warriors who fought several battles without capturing prisoners would disgrace their families. They would be put out of the army and could never wear the warrior's colorful mantles of fine-spun cotton or the distinctive styles of headdress. Ocelotl would have liked to go to war and return with prisoners and treasures, but it never occurred to him to feel sorry for himself because he would, instead, spend his life raising vegetables; if the gods had meant him to be a warrior, he would have been born into a warrior's family. Ocelotl never quarreled with the gods about anything. The less notice they took of him, the better he would like it.

Ocelotl skirted the boat basin beside the canal, which was now filled with the boats of people who had come to market, then he crossed to the northern island, Tlaltelolco. His father and mother had often told him how the people of Tenochtitlán had fought these people of Tlaltelolco, but that was in the past. Now they were one people. As he walked slowly around the plaza, looking critically at the goods displayed in the market here, he had to admit that they were almost as good as those in his own market:

vegetables, clothing, tools and household wares, feather capes, slaves—each was in its proper section.

Ocelotl continued to the west until he stood looking up at a great pyramid. Out of sight at the top was the shrine where he knew Huitzilopochtli, the War God, sat in his glory, adorned with gold, turquoise, pearls, and precious stones, and companioned by an ancient rain god, Tlaloc. Ocelotl could not even imagine what went on in the dim temple up the dizzy flight of steps. To his mind the priests and the gods were equally mysterious beings.

He paused beside a smaller circular temple, the curved doorway of which was the open mouth of a great feathered serpent. This was the temple of Quetzalcoatl, the Fair God who had taught his people many arts and crafts before he disappeared over the Eastern Ocean, promising to return again.

Only priests and penitents were in this temple area. Now and then a girl from the nearby religious school walked past, her eyes modestly cast down to the ground. The young sons of priests came here to study for the priesthood. Through a doorway he caught a glimpse of children who were thin and bore many scars. They were droning over ritual, and he was glad to be outside. He would not mind sweeping the temples or cutting thorns for penitents to stick into themselves, but how dull it would be to spend his days inside walls, memorizing religious rituals, fasting, and sticking maguey thorns in his ears and tongue to please the gods.

"After all," thought Ocelotl virtuously to himself, "*someone* has to raise the food so priests can make offerings to the gods, and the gods will take care of the world."

An unpleasant smell drew his eyes to the skull rack where thousands of human skulls were piled. Ocelotl noticed that the sacrificial block in front of the temple was covered with fresh blood. Perhaps a party of merchants had sacrificed a slave in thanks for a safe journey.

By now the sun was overhead. Ocelotl knew that he must hurry

back to his aunt, who would have finished gossiping and would be collecting her things to go back to Xochimilco. He was in for a good scolding, but it had been worth it.

Near the great palace of Montezuma on the corner of the central plaza of Tenochtitlán, however, Ocelotl's way was blocked by an excited crowd. Now and then the clamor stilled as people pushed together to make way for a chief, his jaguar helmet glittering, his shoulders broadened by bulky cotton armor. The clan leaders had been called to the palace. Why? Ocelotl asked several people what had happened, but no one answered him.

Just then a well-dressed merchant came up to another merchant standing near him and told a story that made Ocelotl's flesh creep.

A swift runner from the coastlands had arrived at the palace that morning, gasping out an unbelievable story of white-skinned men, with hair on their faces, who had appeared over the Eastern Sea in a great floating house with enormous white wings. Whether they were gods, men, or animals, no one at the palace could make out from the story or from pictures which a scribe had hurriedly painted on a cloth. The pictures and words described enormous animals with huge mouths out of which came strange noises. The strangers carried great sticks that exploded with a sound like thunder and could kill from afar; arrows bounced harmlessly off these monsters, the points turned aside by magic. As this story ran through the crowd, many people whispered to one another the old legend of Quetzalcoatl, the Fair God, who had disappeared over the Eastern Ocean, promising to come back some day. But why would the god turn against his own people?

As Ocelotl listened, his mouth open and cold fear running through him, a shadow seemed to pass over the bright sun and to chill shining Tenochtitlán. Hurrying back to join his aunt, Ocelotl could not know that in a few months the powerful capital of the Aztecs would be conquered and that its defenders would fall before the guns of the white men.

The Spanish captain, Hernán Cortés, had the day before, in this year, 1519 A.D., landed with his men and horses at Chalchiuh-cueyan, which he renamed Vera Cruz, or the "True Cross."

AZTEC GOVERNMENT. The Aztec state at the time of the Spanish Conquest was still a federation of clans, headed by a war chief who was taking more and more power to himself. The system was like that of the Indian tribes of North America. Aztec clan divisions became more a matter of geography than of family: an individual belonged to one of the twenty *calpulli*, or clans, according to the particular district in which he lived. At the head of the clans were warrior-nobles. The war chief was selected from one special family. He shared the rule with a chief of civil affairs, who for some reason was called the Snake Woman. These two rulers were advised by a council selected from the nobility.

The famous Aztec law courts probably originated when clan leaders settled land disputes. Four main courts for serious matters were located in Tenochtitlán. In these courts a chief judge and two assistants, chosen from the nobles, passed judgment. Three bailiffs carried out the sentences immediately. A higher court of appeal was located in the ruler's palace. In addition to the civil courts, there were military ones.

SOCIAL ORGANIZATION. As the Aztecs conquered more territory, the earlier clan system changed into a less democratic class society in which there were royal persons, priest-nobles, and warriors; middle-class traders, professional people, and craftsmen; and agricultural workers and slaves. Slavery was common but was not always as bad as we think of its being. Slaves could own homes and property, and they could even own other slaves. Slaves were sometimes free to do their own work after they had put in a certain amount of time for their masters. Prisoners captured in battle, however, suffered a more cruel fate, as we shall see.

The Aztecs, like most other Indians, considered that the earth was common property. Part of the land was set aside to be tilled for the nobility and priests, whose duties left them no time for farming. The rest was divided among the people, by a system which took into account what each farmer needed and could tend. His "lease" ran for a two-year period. If his land was neglected or badly tended, he was given warning. If this happened a second time, his land was taken from him and given to a better farmer.

As time passed, however, the more powerful chiefs began to own great estates. One family grew so powerful that it became "royal"; that is, the supreme ruler was selected from among its members, by appointed electors. Usually the electors chose a brother or cousin of the dead ruler rather than a young son.

The wealth of the Mexica chiefs dazzled the Spanish conquerors, who naturally concluded that these war chiefs were emperors, as their own rulers were. The last "emperor," the war chief Montezuma II, was treacherously put to death by the Spanish after his subjects had collected a roomful of gold for his ransom, but he made a great impression on the conquerors. They reported that he traveled in a litter carried by four chiefs, his royal head shaded by a feather canopy embroidered with gold and silver and set with jewels. Too precious to set his foot on earth, he walked upon a cloth spread down before him. Too sacred to be looked upon by common eyes, he was tended by people who kept their eyes lowered. From his jeweled sandals to his jeweled headdress, Montezuma glittered with treasures that made the Spaniards burn with envy. His way of living was a great contrast to the simplicity of his nomadic ancestors from North America.

But the Mexicas, or Aztecs, like the Toltecs before them, failed to stand together in their hour of crisis and fell prey to a handful of invaders whom they could easily have conquered.

EDUCATION OF THE AZTECS. Aztec life was surrounded with ritual from birth to death. With the baby's first breath, the midwife prayed for the child, after which she warned the newcomer of what he could expect, saying, "Child, more precious than anything, Ometecuhtli and Omecihuatl created you in the twelfth heaven to come to this world and be born here. Know then that this world, which you have entered, is sad, doleful, and full of hard toil and unhappiness. It is a valley of tears, and as you grow up in it, you must earn your sustenance with your hands and at the cost of much sorrow."

Death was the beginning of a long, hard journey upon which the spirit was sped by numerous ceremonies. These rites increased in richness with the rank of the dead man. When a high chief died, many slaves were sacrificed to provide him with service in the afterlife. But when the ruler himself died, several hundred people, including some of his wives and entertainers, were compelled to follow him, however unwillingly, into the spirit world.

In the years between birth and death, life was somewhat more cheerful. At their sixth year the children of the nobles and the well-to-do were sent to boarding schools where they learned history, traditions, religious rituals, and whatever art or craft they were to follow in life. Middle-class boys went to the clan school of their own geographical group, where they were taught by priests. Sons of the nobles attended the *calmecac*, which was the school attached to the main temple section of Tenochtitlán. Here future warriors and priests received the strictest sort of instruction, meanwhile serving as young attendants in the temple of Huitzilopochtli, the War God.

Strict honesty was expected of everyone. Aztec children were brought up very severely, unlike those of most of the American Indian tribes. Whipping with stinging nettles was one form of punishment. For a graver offense, the child might be hung by his heels in the biting smoke over a fire of red peppers. A child who told lies might have a piece cut out of his lip. If the parents decided the case was hopeless, they might even sell the child into slavery. As a result of this upbringing, honesty was general in the Aztec communities; people who left their houses merely placed crossed sticks in the doorway to indicate that they were away, knowing nothing would be stolen in their absence.

AZTEC RELIGION: THE OLD GODS CHANGE. The early Mexicas were deeply religious. Dr. Herbert J. Spinden, who has studied the Indians of Central America for almost a lifetime, says of their gods that ". . . the situation is confused beyond the point of analysis." Yet these people were not entirely different from other human beings, and their gods were not entirely different, either.

Generally speaking, the oldest gods were food providers. Thus, as the culture of corn was developed, before the time of Christ, a religion was built up around that crop. Now what is important to people whose lives depend upon a plant food? Rain and sunshine, the fertility of the soil, the strength of the seed, you may answer. Since women produced children, it seemed likely that an earth-mother goddess maintained the fertility of the soil. Small female idols, carved of stone or shaped of clay, are among the earliest Mexica idols found; they were probably fertility goddesses. A later goddess, Tlazolteotl, has a name which means "Dirt Goddess" or "Heart of the Earth." The ancient mountain gods of rain and water were called the Tlalocs. Other gods and goddesses represented corn at various stages of its growth. Yet the worshipers of these corn gods did not forget the very ancient hunting gods and weather gods of their nomadic ancestors, or the god of fire, whose Aztec name means "The Old Old God."

As the Mexicas changed from farmers to city dwellers, their gods changed too, and the gods of crops and hunting became war gods. Xipe-totec, the Aztec god of human sacrifice, may have once been a corn god; the flaying of his victims may have symbolized the husking of corn. Perhaps he became a war god because his worship came to demand continual human sacrifices, which could only be obtained by war.

Each of the early cities had its own local god. Huitzilopochtli was the War God and special deity of Tenochtitlán, and as Tenochtitlán became powerful, he became dominant over the gods of conquered cities. As the Aztecs took over other cities, they took over the gods of the conquered people. Then the old agricultural gods of the earth took on new names and duties as their worshipers made conquests over other groups. But the city people, who knew more about love than they did about farming, changed one of the fertility goddesses to a love goddess. This same change had occurred with the goddesses of Egypt, of Greece, and of Rome, in the case of an ancient moon goddess who became the classical goddess we know as Venus.

QUETZALCOATL
(The Plumed Serpent God)

HUITZILOPOCHTLI
(The War God)

THE PLUMED SERPENT. Among the Aztecs we find legends of the overthrow of Quetzalcoatl, an older god of the Toltecs, by Huitzilopochtli and other Aztec gods. It is possible that Huitzilopochtli had once been the god of the sword-leaved maguey plant but had become the chief war god by the time of Tenochtitlán. Quetzalcoatl, the great Toltec Plumed Serpent god, had probably been the chief god of the conquered tribes. The legend that Quetzalcoatl taught his people the arts and gave them the calendar may be a faint racial memory of arts that the pre-Aztec people learned from the more cultured Mayan tribes of the south. The circular temples built to Quetzalcoatl may show that he was once a wind god, or perhaps a very ancient god, since round structures preceded square ones in the Americas. In conjunction with the planet Venus, this god was expected to reappear from the East in the Venus year of "I Acatl." The appearance of Cortés on this date was a lucky coincidence for the Spaniards and a most unlucky one for the Mexicas, who at first thought the white conqueror was their own Fair God returned to them.

Worship of the gods occupied the principal place in the life of the Mexicas. Theirs was a religion of cruel sacrifices and self-inflicted penance, based on the idea that by prayers, rites, and the force of example, man could influence nature and animal life.

Corn planting was overlaid with ritual from beginning to end. The seed, the soil, and the elements were addressed with prayers such as, "Listen, Sister Seed, remember that you are our sustenance. And you, Your Highness the Soil, now that I am entrusting into your hands my Sister who gives us our maintenance, take care that you do no wrong." Prayers continued as the plants grew, and candles, copal, and turkeys were sacrificed to the corn gods. When the first green corn was eaten, offerings were made to the Old Old God of fire, Xiuhtecutli, whose worship probably went back to hunting days. Idols made of flour from the first seed were placed on the family altar, together with offerings of flowers, candles, copal, and pulque, a drink made from the juice of the agave plant. These were later consumed, in the spirit communion is taken in the Christian church.

HUMAN SACRIFICE. Despite the confusion of many gods, Aztec high priests, at least, believed that back of everything was an invisible and all-powerful god of Cause. They believed, too, that man had a soul and that forgiveness for his serious sins could be asked only once. It is hard to understand how they justified human sacrifice. Usually the victims of the rites were prisoners captured in war, although slaves and even Aztec children were also sacrificed now and then. The Aztecs had to remain at war in order to get a sufficient number of sacrifices. Mexica warriors were taught that death by sacrifice was the normal and fitting end of a warrior, and that it would ensure an afterlife in which the victim would turn into a hummingbird and accompany Huitzilopochtli.

The usual form of Aztec sacrifice was to tear out the victim's heart and offer it to the gods. Many of the stone tubs into which

the hearts were thrown may be seen today. In 1487, during the dedication of a great temple to Huitzilopochtli, twenty thousand people were sacrificed in this way. Like others of the North American tribes, the Aztecs also practiced an arrow sacrifice; in this the victims were tied to posts around which the celebrants circled, shooting the helpless captives with their arrows. In ceremonies to Xipe-totec, the god of sacrifice, as we have observed, priests skinned the victims, perhaps to symbolize the husking of corn. Sometimes they wore the skin like a suit of clothes for twenty days thereafter.

In thinking about Aztec cruelty, we must remember that conscience usually gives back to the adult the ideas of right and wrong which have been drilled into it during early childhood.

A conscience can be trained to accept cruelty as a righteous religious sacrifice. To the Aztec conscience, the sacrificial murder of prisoners was the way to serve their gods. They believed that the gods had to be fed on human blood and that this was man's repayment for the gods' help. The war god was also a sun god, and the human victims who were sacrificed died to feed the sun.

The Aztecs also believed that at times the god's life needed to be renewed. This may have been suggested by the dying down of vegetation in winter, followed by its rebirth in spring. To renew the god's life, the Aztec priests chose from among the handsomest captured chieftains a young man who was to impersonate the god. He was given rich food and clothing for a year. At the end of the year he was crowned and given wives. Then he was sacrificed with great ceremony, and by his death the god would be renewed.

Such ideas and customs are very old; they were not confined to the Aztecs only but were widespread. The ancestors of the Egyptians, Hebrews, and Greeks once made human sacrifices, but the custom was replaced by substitute sacrifices before historic times. The wonder is not that one Indian group practiced it but that there was so little of it among the other Indians.

Human sacrifice became a vicious circle with the Aztecs. There is evidence that it began in a very small way and increased rapidly during later years, reaching a peak at about the time of the Spanish Conquest. The Toltecs had sacrificed butterflies and birds and on rare occasions had offered up children to the Tlalocs, or rain gods. After the Aztecs conquered the cities in the valley of Mexico and took Quetzalcoatl as one of their own gods, they remembered him as a mild, gentle god of an older time who did not demand human sacrifices.

During their thousand-year wandering from their northern home, the Aztecs had lived poorly and had fought their way, while the corn-growing people in Central America had lived more peaceably. Therefore, the Aztecs, when the white men discovered them, were still a fighting tribe who prized the warlike virtues and worshiped cruel war gods. Yet it may be that the more they fought and made human sacrifices to their gods, the more guilt they felt and the harder they tried to do what they thought the gods wanted. Man is a sociable creature and has never found cruelty to be a good basis for a religion or a civilization.

It must be remembered that the Aztecs fought to take prisoners, so their warfare was not as destructive of human life as if they had set out to kill their enemies in battle. We must remember, also, that our accounts of Aztec human sacrifices come chiefly from the records of horrified Spanish priests. Yet the Inquisition took thousands of lives for every hundred that the Aztecs sacrificed. And, finally, for modern man to condemn the Aztecs would be unjust, since we live in a civilization which in two decades has sacrificed over forty million people to the gods of war, empire, and nationalism.

XII. CHILDREN OF THE SUN

Hymn to Viracocha

O Viracocha, Lord of the Universe,
Whether Thou be male or female
At least lord of heat and generation!

.   .   .

Thou mayest be above,
Thou mayest be below,
Or round about Thy rich throne or staff.
O listen to me!

From the sea above in which Thou mayest dwell,
From the sea below in which Thou mayest be,
Creator of the world,
Maker of man,
Lord of all lords!

.   .   .

The Sun, the Moon
The Day, the Night
Summer, Winter
Not vainly, in proper order,
Do they march to the destined place,
To the end!
They arrive wherever Thy royal staff
Thou bearest.
Hear me!
Heed me!
Let it not happen
That I grow tired,
That I die!

This poem to the creator god worshiped by the peoples of the Indian cultures of the Andes region was said to have been composed by the priest-rulers of the Incas, from whom historians writing shortly after the Conquest took it. It may be a remnant of much earlier religious ritual, taken over along with everything else by the Inca overlords who had so recently conquered the earlier cultures.

The belief in an invisible god who created man was widespread among the American Indians. To this god, ruler of sun, moon, day, night, and the seasons, many of the Indian prayer poems were directed.

CHILDREN OF THE SUN

SOUTH AMERICA was first inhabited by wandering hunters, fishermen, and food gatherers who, like their North American counterparts, advanced but little toward the skills of agriculture and the arts. All the evidence that archaeologists and anthropologists have been able to gather together through years of investigation encourages the belief that these people migrated from the north by way of the Isthmus of Panama, and found their way by slow degrees into almost every part of the huge South American continent. By the time Columbus opened the way for the European conquest of the Americas, the pattern of culture in South America had settled into three general ways of life: the Southern Hunters, the Tropical Agriculturalists, and the Andean Farmers. But on this continent too, as in North America, there were areas in which, by reason of favorable situation and historical contacts, civilization rose to a high peak of development.

Here, in a relatively small territory, there had developed by the time the Spaniards came a culture more splendid than any other on the South American continent, that known to us as the Inca Empire. From the profuse remains found in the Central Andes, archaeologists have been able to reconstruct a detailed and impressive story of an ancient civilization.

Cuzco, Capital of the Incas. Long before the Aztec city of Tenochtitlán had reared its pyramids and palaces on the mud flats of Lake Texcoco, there already existed a great Indian city in a beautiful high valley in the Andes mountains of Peru. This city was so sacred that even to this day the Indians of the region stop in awe when they come in sight of it and salute it as "mighty Cuzco." Cuzco was capital of the Inca realm, which stretched almost two thousand miles along the west coast of South America. It was still a busy center when Columbus discovered America.

The people of Cuzco believed that they were the "Children of the Sun." During the days of the glory of Cuzco, at a certain hour of the morning the sun shone in through a window of the great Temple of the Sun upon a golden and jeweled image of the Sun himself, placed upon a high altar facing east. On golden thrones in a semicircle around the Sun image were the mummies of earlier Inca rulers. In the great temple and in its terraced gardens were golden fountains surrounded by golden models of plants, animals, birds, and insects. In smaller temples nearby, lesser deities were worshiped: the moon, the stars, the thunder, the lightning, and other nature gods.

To some twelve million people in the 380,000 square miles of the Inca domain, Cuzco was the center of the world, as its name signified. From the Sacred Square of this capital four broad, paved highways led across mountain chasms or shifting desert sands to four provinces of the empire. Relays of swift runners brought news to Cuzco from the ends of the realm. Slow llama trains carried corn, wool, gold, silver, and other raw materials to the capital and returned to the provinces laden with objects made by the city craftsmen.

Cuzco, like Rome, was not built in a day. Centuries had gone into the construction of its massive temples and palaces. Yet even in this protected spot the Children of the Sun did not feel safe from their enemies. They built a citadel called Sacsahuaman on a hill that drops off sharply on the outskirts of Cuzco; it was to be used in times of siege. Here builders set enormous stone blocks into a triple line of zigzag walls, cutting and fitting together the stones so skillfully that even a knife blade could not be forced between them. Inside the fortress they built living rooms, stairs, fountains, and reservoirs for water which they siphoned uphill. Cuzco shows that it was built by a race of skillful engineers. Where had the builders come from? Why had they built their city so high in the mountains? Why were they so lonely and hard-pressed?

How We Know About the Early People of the Andes. To answer these and other questions, archaeologists have excavated hundreds of ruins in Peru and Bolivia, and they have also studied ancient Indian legends which were preserved orally or written down by the Spanish conquerors. The people of the Andes, early and late, had no written language. By the time of the Incas, detailed records were kept by priests with trained memories, aided by reminders called "quipus," made of knotted colored cords. Colors and knots, as well as pebbles and grains of corn, stood for certain figures, their position near the end or the beginning of the cord showing whether the figures were in tens or hundreds. These quipu records were used for counting the number of citizens, the taxes they paid, the hours they put into road building and other public works, and the goods they produced and received. More elaborate quipus served as memory aids to the priests trained to preserve tribal history and religious songs and rituals. The quipus might have told us much about the Incas, but the Spanish burned the quipu libraries, and the secret of reading the historical records died.

So what we know about the people of the Andes comes from archaeological studies of ancient ruins and from Inca legends, as well as from historical accounts, and religious rituals written down by Spanish priests. The Incas believed that their tribe was descended from two Children of the Sun God, Manco Capac and his sister Mama Ocllo. The Sun had sent these two to Cuzco from Lake Titicaca, which lies on the border between Bolivia and Peru. They had been instructed to settle at the spot where a golden rod carried by Manco Capac would be drawn down into the ground. The pair traveled down the steep mountainsides from the high plateau through chasms cut by rivers. Here and there they paused to test the ground with the golden rod. At the spot where the rod at last disappeared into the earth, the royal pair settled to found Cuzco and the Inca dynasty. Other legends speak of early people of the Lake Titicaca region, overpowered by invaders from the south, and of a few who escaped to Tampu Tocco, another early Inca stronghold in the Andes mountains.

PRE-INCAIC PEOPLES OF THE COAST. Archaeologists say that Cuzco was, in truth, founded by refugees from a much older culture at Lake Titicaca. At least three centers of pre-Incaic culture are known to have existed along the coast. They are at Chan Chan, at Pachacamac, and in the Nasca valley.

Let us take a bird's-eye view of these regions and see why different customs and arts grew up in them. To fly across the ancient Inca state takes almost two days. The air traveler wonders how an army on foot could ever have covered so much difficult country. The plane from the north crosses the equator in its name-sake country Ecuador, and passengers look down on green jungles broken only by lazy rivers. Soon, however, they are flying over the yellow sands of the coastal desert of Peru—a desert created by the Andes mountains as they rose and cut off trade winds blowing westward from the distant Atlantic.

Here and there the coastal desert is cut by green valleys, made by rivers running from the mountains to the sea. Halfway between the equator and Lima, Peru, one flies over the ruins of the city called Chan Chan, where, shortly after the time of Christ, there lived a highly artistic group of Indians called the Chimus. Far southward are the ruins of Pachacamac, some eighteen miles past Lima, the modern Peruvian capital. Still farther south are the remains of the irrigation canals that watered the once populous Nasca valley.

These early coastal people, who had irrigated desert stretches to make gardens, were conquered by the tribes from the high tableland of the Andes and became part of the Inca state that still flourished when America was discovered.

Cieza de León, a Spanish soldier and conquistador, wrote that in Peru there were three regions where men could "nowise exist." One was the dense rain forest south of the Andes. The second was the intensely cold sierra region of the high Andes. The third was the sandy desert, where nothing could be seen but sand hills scourged by a fierce sun. In between these uninhabitable regions, wrote the old soldier, there were fertile valleys where many people once lived, in cities that are now in ruins. Today we know more about these cities than the Spanish soldier knew.

CHAN CHAN OF THE CHIMUS. One of the most interesting of those ancient cities was Chan Chan, capital of the Chimu people who lived in the broad Chicama-Moche valley of northwestern Peru. Chan Chan was a great city at the time of the fall of Rome.

Today the air traveler looks down on row upon row of ruins that mark out temples and palaces, walled-in gardens, dams, and lakes.

Now all is desert, but fifteen hundred years ago Chan Chan must have been beautiful, with its houses of sun-baked clay, painted in dazzling colors, and its vine-hung balconies set in terraced gardens. Tree-bordered lakes were fed by canals, some of which had sixty-foot embankments. The ruins of Chan Chan stretch out to an extent which would make ancient Troy seem like a village; archaeologists have called it the Babylon of the Americas. The central part of the city was several miles square. Beyond lay suburban areas large enough to be called towns. The divisions of the city suggest that its people were grouped into clans occupying separate quarters, a common Indian custom.

No one knows how many people lived in Chan Chan. Earlier archaeologists estimated that they numbered several hundred thousand. It may be, however, that Chan Chan was not so much a great residential city as it was a fairground used at intervals for commercial and religious meetings. Its products are found several hundred miles along the Peruvian coast and some fifty miles inland. The splendor of its ruler, known as the Grand Chimu, was so dazzling that legends about him have remained alive among the Indians of the region to this day.

During religious festivals throughout the heyday of Chan Chan, the city was crowded with thousands upon thousands of Indians from the Andes and the coast, who thronged to the temples with their offerings of flowers, food, and funeral pottery. On market days people from far and near brought their vegetables and fruits, pottery, textiles, and other products here, just as their brightly dressed descendants crowd the plazas of Andean towns on market days even now.

Chan Chan fell to destruction long before the Incas swept into the valley of the Moche. The Chimus left no written records, yet we know exactly how they looked and how they lived. We learn this from the ceramics they put into tombs of their dead. Like the ancient Egyptians, the Chimus overlooked no detail that would serve to keep the departed spirit in touch with the facts of daily life. Rich man, poor man, beggarman, warrior, cripple, musician, people at work, people at play, people making love, people asleep at their work: Chimu potters modeled and painted them so faithfully that a camera could hardly have shown us more clearly how they looked. No more fascinating record of an ancient people exists than the Chimu ceramics, which may be seen in the Peruvian Archaeological Museum at Lima.

Fortunately for us, this pottery did not interest the thieves who for centuries plundered Chimu graves of precious stones, gold cups, masks, spoons, necklaces and earrings, and other treasures buried with the dead rulers.

On down the coast, eighteen miles past modern Lima, was Pachacamac, another seaside center that flourished long before the Incas. Enormous temples, and more graveyards than one city could be expected to fill, show that Pachacamac was also a religious center where people came to worship and in whose sacred grounds they buried their dead. When the Spanish conquistador, Pedro de Cieza de León, first saw the great temple there, its adobe walls still showed traces of painted animals. He reported that the people of this valley had been conquered by the Incas only after four years of fighting. The conquerors had not destroyed the temple or interfered with the religious rites, he wrote, but had set aside "the loftiest part" as a temple to the Sun God. In this irrigated valley, he continued, corn was planted deep in the earth, with small fish to fertilize it.

The people of the Nasca valley still farther south had also irrigated the desert to make it bloom. The Nascas were very skilled at making textiles and ceramics, although they did not model portrait vases like those of the Chimus of Chan Chan.

PRE-INCAIC PEOPLES OF THE HIGHLANDS. The sierra, the mountain region that rises back of the Peruvian desert, also produced early cultures. The chief of these was centered at Tiahuanaco, which, in the language spoken by the Incas, means "City of the Dead." The ruins of Tiahuanaco are on a barren plateau thirteen thousand feet above sea level at the southern end of Lake Titicaca in Bolivia. Tiahuanaco was the center of a mountain civilization at the same time that the Chimus and other early people lived in cities on the coast. Its courtyards and gateways were built of enormous blocks of stone, usually carved with the faces of their gods. The "Gateway of the Sun" stands more than thirteen feet high and is more than seven feet wide. Carved on its stones are Viracocha, the Creator God, and twenty-four attendant gods.

The culture which archaeologists call Tiahuanaco I began about 600 B.C. and ended about 500 A.D. For several centuries its products were widespread from southern Ecuador to northern Argentina.

Some time about 1000 A.D., an unknown disaster scattered the people of Tiahuanaco. Was it earthquake, famine, disease, or an invasion of barbarian tribes from the southwest?

The many ruins make it clear that at one time thousands of people lived in this region. What happened to them? Such a large population would have required enormous supplies of corn or other foods, yet today corn will not ripen on this high plateau. Furthermore, how could people working in such thin mountain air have moved such heavy blocks of stone? An English geologist has given us a possible explanation of these mysteries and of the disaster that befell Tiahuanaco. He points out that the Andes, a young mountain range still pushing upward, may have risen a thousand feet since Tiahuanaco was built. During this rise, winters have grown longer and colder and summers shorter and cooler. While this slow, unnoticed elevation of the plateau was taking place, and as the corn-ripening season grew shorter each year and there was less and less to eat, the people of Tiahuanaco must have felt that the gods had turned against them.

Added to this slow disaster there may have been an invasion of barbaric tribes, as legends suggest. Whatever the reason, the Tiahuanaco people scattered in search of better living conditions. The ancestors of the Incas left the Titicaca basin on a journey that ended in Cuzco. Here they began the great period of Andean culture, the Incaic, which lasted from 1200 until the destruction of the Incas by Spanish conquerors.

You may wonder if these early town builders of the Andes and the coast borrowed corn culture and other ideas from the pre-Mayan people. Archaeologists find a few South American words which also appear in old Central American languages, suggesting some contact between the two regions. Such contact must have been before the time of Christ. Only after 1000 A.D. do Mayan evidences appear in South America.

Certainly the pre-Incaic people of Peru developed the potato and other valuable foods. They terraced mountainsides and built elaborate drainage systems and remarkable roads. Their weaving and metalworking have scarcely ever been excelled. Their religious thought was also remarkable, for they believed in one all-powerful "Uncreated Creator," but since they did not have the Mayan habit of erecting carved stone markers, we do not know when this god first appeared. This god, known as Pachacamac to the coastal people and as Viracocha to the Incas, was recognized as the all-powerful, all-knowing creator of the universe. The pre-Incaic people of the coastal towns also worshiped various other gods and goddesses of the earth, sea, and sky.

The archaeological discoveries at Tiahuanaco explain the legend that ancestors of the Incas were the Children of the Sun, who had been sent down to Cuzco from their home at Lake Titicaca. Inca rulers were later to justify their conquests by saying that they were sent to earth to bring order to all people. A sturdy and aggressive people, the Incas took over the agricultural and mechanical skills of the older civilization. Within a short period they made themselves the master race of the Andes, conquering an area which extended some two thousand miles in length. To their credit it must be said that at their best the Incas ruled with a stern sort of social justice that provided physical care not only for their own people but also for those whom they conquered. We shall study the Inca form of government in some detail, as the extreme form of undemocratic efficiency developed in Indian America, which for the most part held to a simple tribal organization.

How New Territories Were Brought into the Inca State. Some of the Inca rulers were admirable, others merely despots, but each carried out a successful plan for bringing conquered people into the Inca state. Unlike the Aztecs, the Inca armies did not capture prisoners for sacrifice, nor did they impose a harsh system of taxes. The conquering army was followed by census takers who made records of the population and of the crafts, products, and work that might be expected of the area. The conquered territory was divided and its former rulers were moved to Cuzco. After a training period among the splendors of the Inca capital, they returned to govern their former territories for the Incas. Their children remained in Cuzco, to be educated in Inca ways and to serve as hostages for the good behavior of their fathers.

The local gods of the conquered people were also conducted to Cuzco with great ceremony, where they took places secondary to the Inca deities. Temples to the Sun God were set up in the conquered territory, in charge of priests whose duty it was to make converts of the conquered people. The Incas did not ban the native languages or the ancient customs of the conquered provinces, but since they obliged the people to learn Quechua as the official language, this soon replaced the original tongues.

The Inca authority was not to be questioned. At the least sign of trouble, the Inca's soldiers would move thousands of people to a part of the country where they would be among strangers who would not join them in rebellion. Besides the rebellious ones, there were three other classes of "displaced people." First were the herdsmen who were sent up the mountains to tend the flocks of the Inca rulers, and the craftsmen sent to teach conquered tribes how to make ornaments and other products. A second class of displaced persons were those who could be trusted to man the garrisons scattered throughout the Inca area. A third class were loyal Incas sent to settle uninhabited valleys or those sent to conquered territories to teach the Quechua language and Inca customs. So, by a combination of force and education, the conquered became citizens of the state and lived under the same strict and efficient system by which the Inca's own people were ruled.

THE INCA STATE. For purposes of administration, the land ruled by the Inca was divided into four quarters, with Cuzco at the center. Each province had its own capital city ruled by a governor from the royal family and was itself divided into quarters. Each quarter was again quartered and ruled by an official responsible directly to the Inca. Eight main ranks of officials, all relatives of the ruler, were in charge of the Inca population. This system was made possible by the fact that every Inca had many children, by different wives, so that each ruler had innumerable uncles and cousins, who were trained to be administrators. The chief ruler was called "The Only Inca" and might have said, "I am the State." His authority was not limited by clan representatives, as was the case with the Aztec chief. Below the Inca nobles were two ranks: the nobles of conquered tribes, and the common people. The common people had no representatives and no contact with the ruler except on those occasions when he visited the provinces, giving audience with great pomp and ceremony. Even then they could not even raise their eyes to look at the Inca or enter his presence with shoes on.

The magnificence of The Only Inca was unequaled, since he claimed title to all the gold, silver, and precious jewels of the country. When an Inca died, his palaces were sealed off and his treasures buried with him. Thus each new ruler had to collect his own treasure. Some rulers had as many as two hundred palaces, which, according to Spanish observers, were ablaze with gold and jewels. A hall in one palace was said to hold four thousand people.

The ruler was considered the human form of the god. The High Priest, a brother of the Inca, controlled the priesthood, appointing other members of the family to the various religious offices below his own. Such a state, where the human ruler is believed to be the god himself, is called a "theocracy," a word which means "god-ruled." The Inca theocracy was much like that of ancient Egypt, with its Pharaohs who were thought to be the incarnation of the gods. Such a type of government, like any dictatorship, concentrates wealth and power in a few hands and makes the common people little more than slaves.

It sometimes happens, however, that the small ruling minority develops a sense of real responsibility and leadership, and such was the case with some of the Inca rulers. Boys of the royal family were trained from infancy to be dependable, honest, courageous, and efficient. The future ruler and his royal kinsmen were given harsh training in fighting, fasting, exposure to cold, and in stiff contests of skill and endurance. They were taught to interpret the quipu records and to carry on the details of government. The Inca soil-conservation program made it possible to feed more people than can be supported in the same area today.

As usually happens in such a state, the education of girls was limited to domestic training. Girls of the nobility went into convents, where they tended sacred fires and wove royal robes for the Inca, who wore each garment only once. They also made sacrificial garments to be burned at the temple altars or thrown into the river that flowed through Cuzco. Some of these girls became the wives of the Inca. Others were set apart for sacrifice, though human sacrifice was not as common among the Incas as among the Aztecs.

Below the Inca there was the second-class nobility made up of the ex-rulers of conquered territories; beneath these, and set apart from them by dress, dialect, and training, were the common people, organized down to the last infant in arms. Census gatherers divided the people of each district into groups according to age and ability and assigned work on the basis of skill and strength. The most careful records were kept of the supplies given out and the products obtained.

INCA FEUDALISM. The Inca economic system was as efficient as the political system. All lands belonged to the state. Farm land was divided into three parts, one for the Inca, one for the Sun (that is, for the upkeep of temples and the priesthood), and a third for the people. The people's land was divided among the families according to their social rank and the number of their children. Needless to say, the common people did the actual farming. Workers tilled the lands of the Sun first, beginning this religious service with ceremonial music and chants. Next they worked the lands of absent soldiers, of the old, the sick, and the

widowed. Then they were free to plant their own crops, after which they tended those of the Inca.

Industries were carried on in much the same way. Llama wool was gathered into central storehouses, from which it was given out to textile workers who spun it into yarn and wove the yarn into cloth. Corn, potatoes, and other foods were similarly collected, to be given out when needed. Products such as cloth were distributed according to a strict plan. Everyone worked and no one lacked the necessities of life.

THE LOT OF THE COMMON PEOPLE UNDER THE INCAS. You may wonder how well this system worked. The people of the Inca state were fed and clothed; nobody starved or went without clothes or worried about his old age. The common people did not have the freedom we take for granted. They had no free speech, no freedom of religious worship, little freedom of movement, and few civil rights. Traveling was limited to official business. No one could change his occupation or improve his lot. No Inca boy could hope to progress, as our American phrase has it, "from log cabin to president."

The common people received no education. As one Inca ruler said: "It is not proper that commoners should be taught the sciences that belong to the noble, and to him alone, lest the lower class should climb a degree higher or become unduly haughty, mocking or insulting the republic; it is sufficient that they learn their ancestral trades, for it is not for commoners to direct and govern, and to give them this right is to endanger the administration and also the republic."

CRIME AND PUNISHMENT. It never occurred to the Incas that the common people had a right to live as they pleased: they belonged to the ruler and to the clan. Even the patient Indians could not always fit into such a system, but at the slightest trace of rebellion the most severe punishments were inflicted. If a town revolted against the Inca, it was promptly destroyed. If a man cursed the

Sun or the Inca, the words of the curse were likely to be his last words. To take another man's life, property, or wife was punishable by death. To move land boundaries or to divert irrigation streams was a serious crime.

The people had no legal protection, such as they had under the Aztec judiciary system, with its trained judges, common courts, and higher court of appeals. A much less democratic system existed in Peru. To keep check on government officials, spies called "guardians" or "informers" reported to The Only Inca, bringing charges against whatever officials they found to be unjust or dishonest.

Pacha-cutec, one of the greatest of Inca rulers, expressed with dignity certain Inca moral principles, such as the following which an early Spanish historian recorded:

He that kills another without authority or just cause condemns himself to death.

Judges who secretly receive gifts from suitors ought to be looked upon as thieves and punished with death as such.

The physician herbalist who is ignorant of the virtues of herbs or who, knowing the uses of some, has not attained to a knowledge of all, understands little or nothing. He ought to work until he knows all, as well the useful as the injurious plants, in order to deserve the name to which he pretends.

He who attempts to count the stars, not even knowing how to count the marks and knots of the quipus, ought to be held in derision.

Drunkenness, anger, and madness go together; but the first two are voluntary and to be removed, whereas the last is perpetual.

Those moral principles were no real protection to the people, since they were little more than an attempt by autocratic rulers to pacify a people who may still have remembered traditions of the democracy of a clan system.

THE EFFECT OF INCA RULE. People living under such an autocracy could not develop art and literature. The Incas learned the crafts of earlier peoples, and, since craftsmanship and engineering can be carried out efficiently under a dictatorship, they continued to be skillful in these ways. Poets, philosophers, artists, and musicians, however, seldom develop among people allowed no personal freedom. Inca architecture remained crude, without beauty beyond that of massive grandeur. No written language was developed. A few Inca prayers to the gods have remained, however, as evidence that poetry was not entirely crushed out of the souls of the people. The Incas produced no sculpture or painting to compare with those of the Mayas or of the earlier peoples of Peru. Their pottery, though sturdy and useful, did not compare with the wonderful portrait vases made by the Chimus almost a thousand years earlier. Inca sculptors did not improve upon the art found in the bas reliefs of Tiahuanaco. Inca woven designs were usually imitations of earlier textiles, showing little, if any, development

INCA ART

Upper, left and right: designs from Peruvian tapestries; lower, left and right: pottery water jars of the early Chimu period; lower, center: Mochica portrait vessel.

over the marvelous cloths with which the mummies in the coastal graveyards were swathed.

The Inca system for the conservation of land was directed toward saving every yard of fertile soil and terracing mountainsides to the last foot. According to John Collier, in *Indians of the Americas*, it has been estimated by United States Soil Conservation Services that, at 1936 prices, the construction of their terraces would have cost thirty thousand dollars an acre. By a system of public work, the Incas managed to prevent soil erosion—that enemy that has destroyed so many ancient empires, has made a wasteland of Spain, and is creating a future desert in our own dust bowl. Inca rulers would have been horrified by our waste of topsoil.

THE END OF THE INCAS. Like the Roman empire, the Inca state stretched so far that at last it broke into two parts. An Inca named Huayna Capac set up a northern capital at Quito and a southern one at Cuzco. These were ruled respectively by two of the Inca's sons, Atahualpa and Huáscar. After the death of their father, the half brothers began a bloody civil war, which ended only when Atahualpa conquered Cuzco and put some two hundred of his royal half brothers, sisters, and other relatives to a cruel death.

Atahualpa's triumph was cut short in 1534 by the arrival of the Spanish conqueror, Francisco Pizarro. After collecting an immense ransom for which he had promised the Inca his freedom, Pizarro treacherously put Atahualpa to death. The common people had long since had all their courage ground out of them. Without human liberty and personal responsibility, they had become slaves, and when The Only Inca was kidnaped, his subjects did not rescue him. The Inca state was crushed like an eggshell, and its vast treasures flowed back to enrich Spain. The enslaved population passed to the white man's rule, under which it experienced a terror and exploitation far surpassing anything the Incas had ever dreamed of.

XIII: AN END AND A BEGINNING

THE MIGRATION TO THE AMERICAS. We have seen how a new continent was settled by wandering hunters who drifted in from man's old Eurasian home, and how, over thousands of years, these people wandered across the cold top of the world, following the hope of better hunting land beyond. Women burdened with

228

babies, tired children trudging behind, men with only their spears to help them conquer the New World—they must have moved by slow stages across the frozen tundra and on across the natural land bridge which spanned the Bering Strait. Through this gateway between Asia and America, hunting bands found their way in a slow stream beginning perhaps as early as twenty thousand years ago. Down the wide roadway of the Great Plains they followed the animal herds in their migrations.

In the valleys of the New World the first bands of invaders vanished like the smoke of their campfires. Later groups struggled on and made a New World of their own.

Pushed southward by the cold breath of an ice age some ten thousand years ago, the people who made the Folsom spears camped along the streams of the Southwest at a time when lands now desert were fertile plains. They hunted horses, camels, mastodons, and other ice-age animals, and, like those animals, they came to some mysterious end with the change to a warmer climate.

Later arrivals continued to pour across the Bering land or ice bridge and down the great plateau into the valley of Mexico. Then across the narrow land bridge at Panama they made their way, leaving footprints in ancient lava flows in South America.

In a thousand valleys the people of the New World built their villages. With age-long patience they tasted and tested the usefulness of every leaf, root, berry, or fruit of the Americas, learning what was good, what was death, what was healing, what soothed the sufferer or brought strange, colorful dreams. Before the time of Christ, some of them had found, perhaps in the highlands of Central America, a grass with a sweet, yellow seed. Through centuries they saved its grain, planted and tended it, and, with the strength and security given them by corn, they began to build cities.

IMPERIAL DAYS. Architects, sculptors, and painters of these cities learned to produce amazingly beautiful temples, using only simple tools of stone. In Central and South America villages grew into city-states and city-states into virtual empires, not once but several times.

The Mayas built and abandoned templed cities in Guatemala, in southern Mexico, and in Yucatán. Mayan priests kept records of the movements of the stars and planets over many centuries and made a calendar more accurate than that used by our own ancestors in Europe at the same time.

Pre-Aztec people had spread into the tropics from their cities in the valley of Mexico, bringing back bright feathers and other ornaments for brilliant ceremonies in their temples atop their towering pyramids. Centuries afterwards, Aztec armies went out from their city Tenochtitlán to conquer much of what is now Mexico.

Long before the Aztecs, the pre-Incaic people of the high Andes mountains had cultivated the potato. They had built enormous stone temples and fortresses and had terraced mountains to make fields which they watered by means of vast irrigation projects. Much later, the Inca tribes built a highly organized state upon this older agricultural base.

Meanwhile, new arrivals from Asia poured into the vast spaces of North America to plunder the harvests of early corn planters of the Southwest, who retired to cliff dwellings and defended their holdings for thousands of years. They were defeated now and then by conquerors who then blended with the older stock and became town dwellers themselves. Other tribes with poorer food reserves and less favorable sites for strongholds were washed over time after time by fresh waves of nomadic invaders from the north.

Before the Vikings had touched on American shores, there had also been invasions of North America from the south. Ideas, art forms, and religious ceremonies spread in some way across the Gulf of Mexico and up the valleys of the Mississippi and the Ohio river systems, to appear as a dim reflection of Mayan glories. Thousands of temple mounds were piled up. Arts and crafts flourished in Mound Builder villages for several centuries and then disappeared.

The first Americans tried almost all of the known forms of social life and government. We could learn much from their successes and their failures. Usually the Indians lived a simple, democratic life, with the group led by its strongest and wisest men. The military dictatorships and state socialism of the highly populated areas of South America were the exception rather than the rule.

FALL OF INDIAN AMERICA. The sword of the European cut across this great experiment of a new race in a new world. Even the great Indian states of Central and South America fell before a handful of Spaniards. There are several reasons why this happened. One factor was the hardihood of the Spanish and Portugese invaders. The conquistadors were as strong and tough as their sword blades forged at Toledo. Like their own steel, they had been fused from the strongest elements and forged in the hottest fires.

The Iberian peninsula guards the entrance to the Mediterranean. It is the end of European roads and the bridge to ancient man's hunting grounds in the enormous continent of Africa. The ablest and most adventurous men left their traces on these ancient crossroads. Twenty thousand years before Christ, Cro-Magnon artists made their superb paintings upon Spanish cave walls. In later days the peninsula was colonized by the strongest and most intelligent peoples of the ancient world: Minoans, Phoenicians, and Greeks.

Spain was a military outpost of Imperial Rome and gave to Rome its most admirable late emperor, Marcus Aurelius. While the rest of Europe moved slowly through the Dark Ages when learning was almost forgotten, Spain was a center of the rich and dazzling Mohammedan culture which, in the eighth century A.D., spread like wildfire across northern Africa, Arabia, and eastward through Persia to India. When Ferdinand and Isabella drove the Moors from Spain shortly before the discovery of America, centuries of Moorish toughness were already well set in Spanish blood and character.

Thousands of years of such crosscurrents of struggle and culture made the sixteenth-century Spaniard the toughest, most intense, and most fanatical of individualists. He carried a sword in one hand and a cross in the other. Adventurers and crusaders alike would dare anything for "gold, God, and Spain." The best of them were brilliant, fearless, and imaginative. The worst, common riffraff adventurers, were hardy and tireless.

The white man came with startling swiftness across the Eastern Sea. He appeared before the Indian in his shining armor, riding an enormous four-footed creature such as had not been seen in the Americas, since the horses had become extinct here some twelve thousand years before Christ. The Indians thought that the horse, the man, and the gun were one creature, a god whom Indian spears could not kill. The Spaniards, learning of this belief, craftily buried their dead under cover of night, so that the Indians would not know that their enemies were only other mortals like themselves.

The handful of Spaniards could have been overpowered by the sheer weight of Aztec or Inca armies, made up of brave fighters who were skilled in warfare. But superstition worked for the white men and against the Indians. The legend that hastened the Indians' undoing was that of the Fair God, who, in the distant past of the Mayan and the pre-Aztecan peoples, had taught them the arts and crafts, then had said farewell and had departed over the Eastern Sea, promising to return again to lead his people. He left behind his symbol, the plumed serpent, which, as bird and serpent, was the symbol of the rain-giving sky and the food-giving earth. The predicted time of the return of this god fell at the ending of a certain period of the calendar based on the planet Venus. As luck would have it, the Spaniards appeared at just this fateful time. Montezuma, the Aztec ruler, had brooded long over the prophecy of the return of the Fair God. Priest and mystic as well as war chief, Montezuma was not one to challenge the greatest god of his race. But while he hesitated, fearing the white man might be the god returned, Cortés had allied himself with the other Mexican tribes who were enemies of the Aztecs, and had reached the outskirts of Tenochtitlán, the Aztec capital.

In this book we cannot tell the story of the overthrow of the Indian cultures, which fell one by one before the ruthless invaders, but it is worth while to consider briefly some of the reasons why they fell. No matter how they might have resisted, in the end the Indians would surely have been conquered, for weapons of wood and stone were no match for iron, steel, and gunpowder. But they fell, unnecessarily, to a handful of invaders, because the various tribes had been fighting one another and did not join together for defense against their common enemy.

When the Spaniards destroyed the Aztec, Mayan, and Inca rulers, they destroyed the brains that might have led the Indian resistance. Where the common people know only how to obey the ruler, there is no possibility of resistance after the ruling class is destroyed.

The Aztec rulers of Mexico fell partly because of their earlier cruelty. The coastal tribes hated the Aztecs because their captured warriors had been sacrificed by the thousands to Aztec war gods. Therefore they were willing to join Cortés against the Aztecs. As the Spaniards advanced, the Aztec priests became more frenzied and sacrificed more victims. Then the Indians saw that, for all the thousands of human lives sacrificed, the Indian war gods were unable or unwilling to protect their worshipers. With their faith in their gods weakened, the ground was taken from under the feet of the defenders.

For the same reasons, the Inca state in South America was not defended by its recently conquered subject tribes. Although the Inca conquests had been entirely different from Aztec warfare, and human sacrifice had no part in it, the stern socialistic state did not have the support of the common people in its hour of crisis. The absolute rule of the priest-nobility had sapped the strength of the people and killed their ability to think and to act. When their rulers, who had been considered far too sacred to be looked upon by common eyes, were seen to be powerless before the strange white gods, the common people felt themselves to be helpless.

The Mayan civilization of Central America was already half destroyed by agricultural breakdown and civil war when the conquerors came. Like the city-states of the ancient Greeks, the Mayan city-states were divided by local prejudices and ancient feuds. Centuries of civil war had not prepared the Mayas, for all their intelligence, to see that it was necessary for them to unite in the face of a common disaster.

Perhaps the greatest shock, however, was that the Indian had never before faced an enemy so unlike himself. War and disaster he could stand, but when the white man struck down his magic and destroyed his confidence in his own weapons and in his gods, it was a death blow. The climax came when the invader appeared at the prophetic hour when the long-awaited Fair God was expected. By the time that the Indian had discovered that the white man was neither a god nor invulnerable, the damage was done and the invader was successfully entrenched.

The Indian had lived a life that was deeply religious. Through his ceremonies and rites, each man took part in the great processes of nature. He fed and worshiped the gods, who, in turn, gave him rain and sun, nourished his crops, and guided his fate from birth to death. When his magic and his gods failed to stop the white invader, the Indian was not able to give up his belief in magic and in religion; he could only conclude that the white man's magic and his gods were more powerful than were his own.

If the Indian tribes had said, "We are men and brave warriors; we are all one race and will fight together to defend our land against the invader," they might have held their continent for some time longer against a divided Europe. But few peoples have ever been able to give up local prejudices and sovereignty, even in the face of disaster. We of the modern world have not yet done so.

WHAT HAPPENED THEN? The failure of the Indian to hold his continent was followed by an almost incredible story of treachery, murder, and destruction. The Indian states went down in the sixteenth century, and the long, slow misery of the Spanish and Portuguese colonial rule of Central and South America began. In some areas the Indians were totally destroyed; in others, they blended with the white colonists.

There were brave, wise, and good men on both sides. Here and there the black record of the Conquest is lightened. A noble-born Spaniard, Friar Bartolomé de Las Casas, shines like a beacon for his heroic attempts to win freedom for the Indian and for his courageous exposure of the horrors of Spanish rule. Man's one duty is the development of his spirit, said Las Casas, and this development cannot take place except in a free, cooperative commonwealth. Las Casas pleaded passionately with the Crown to keep adventurers, soldiers, and religious fanatics out of the Americas and to allow priests to bring the American multitudes to God, and thus bring Spain to greatness. But Las Casas could not stem the tide of the Spanish lust for gold and empire; the Indian civilizations went down before it, and in time it wrecked the mother country as well.

There is little to choose between the Spanish record in Central and South America and that of our own ancestors who colonized North America. The under-organized Indian tribes of the area in which we live were ruthlessly pushed back by the white men, and their land was taken over even more completely than in Central and South America.

The white conquerors might have learned much from the races they conquered, but they chose to take tangible things. They took the treasures of gold and precious stones which they stripped from the temples and palaces, and they took the food plants the Indians had developed: corn, potatoes, cocoa, beans, squash, pumpkin, and manioc, as well as tobacco, rubber, quinine, and many other plant products. In Central and South America the white conquerors enslaved the Indians by the millions, working them to death in thousands of gold and silver mines, rubber jungles, and haciendas, or great agricultural estates.

In North America there were few treasures, but there was the land. The white man made treaties, which he later tossed aside as "scraps of paper" when the settlers multiplied and called for more room. Indian leaders who protested against this treatment were called to Washington to "conferences," with safety promised them, and then were only too often thrown into jails where they were kept for years, leaving their people leaderless.

Tribes were driven on death marches from their lands to distant areas which were little better than concentration camps. Every effort was made to destroy the Indians' social and religious patterns. This is a story every American should know, for the sake of our national conscience, and it is a story that few of our history books tell.

Today, under an enlightened and far-seeing Indian Administration, our Indians enjoy their proper rights as human beings, though they have not as yet all achieved the exercise of full citizenship. This new policy has already produced a quick and joyous upsurge of art and community cooperation among the Indians, although their problems are far from solved.

WHAT IS LEFT OF THE INDIAN CIVILIZATIONS? Perhaps from the

strength of the Indian we later Americans could learn a way of life, and from his tragedy a needed lesson. His strength lay in social and religious patterns in which every person had a place as a part of a spiritual world as large as all of nature.

The fatal weakness of the Indian of 1492, as we have seen, was his inability to lay aside his local prejudices, his local gods, his local sovereignty, and to join hands with those who might have been his allies in the time of crisis. This weakness destroyed the Indian civilizations, as it may those of the modern world. When the invader came with his policy of "divide and rule," Indian America was chipped away bit by bit and so was destroyed.

The Indian empires had failed to develop responsible democratic human beings able to assume leadership in the face of stunning disaster. Trained armies and a highly skilled ruling class were not enough to make up for this lack. Masses who had lost the sense of their own value could not stand up against even a few men as ruthless and self-confident as the Spaniards. Among the more democratic hunting tribes of North America, there were the same weakening tribal wars and the same inability to forget local quarrels and to unite for a common defense. Without a greater sense of brotherhood, democracy within the tribe was not enough.

Yet the Indian virtues were great ones. Tribal rituals used over thousands of years made it clear to the young Indian that a time came when he must put away childish habits and conform to the demands of society that he fill his role with courage and skill. The Indian was almost fanatically honest: throughout the entire record of the conquest of the Americas we see again and again that the Indian kept his word, only to be betrayed by the white conquerors. Within the tribe, his life was extremely cooperative; our private ownership of land and the concentration of wealth in the hands of a few people were foreign to his general pattern of life, appearing only here and there where the city civilizations existed. For every individual was important to the life of his tribe. It seemed clear to the Indian that the tribe and the individual had to nourish each other and that both had to take part in a life-giving ritualistic union with the higher powers.

What the Indians needed was what every race needs in its hour of crisis: the flexibility to put aside local selfish prejudices and interests, to see a neighbor's danger as one's own, to be willing to sacrifice something of isolated pride in order to unite with others for the common good. Secure in the world he had made for himself, but lacking this flexibility, the red man was destroyed by the invader.

Yet sometimes a tree that has been cut does not die but sends up shoots that grow into new trees. And sometimes men graft upon a sturdy sapling the buds of a more richly yielding tree, so the two will grow into a new tree with the strength of the native stock and the fruit of the highly developed one. Something of this sort often happens when people of one culture conquer those of another. It happened to the Greeks, the Romans, the Spaniards, the English, and the Americans. It may be happening in Latin America, in areas where descendants of the Indians and their conquerors have blended. The Indian-Spanish blend has produced a wonderful renaissance of art and poetry in Mexico and elsewhere in Latin America.

The Indian story is by no means ended. These truly American people who were the real discoverers of America are not only a part of our country's past but will also play a significant role in the drama of its future.

Christopher Columbus misnamed this race "Indians," and it was not until his fourth and last voyage across the Sea of Darkness that, cruising at the mouth of the Orinoco River, he realized that he had not found the Golden Chersonese, the Strait of Malacca, that would lead to the wealth of India, but that he had discovered a New World. He wrote:

I am convinced that this is a mainland, very large, unknown heretofore, and reason helps me greatly on account of this great river and sea, which is fresh; and then I draw help also from the saying of Esdras that six parts of the earth are dry and one under water, a book approved of by Saint Ambrose and Saint Augustine.

Seeing this river of sweet water that flowed out of the green land in the straits of the Dragon's Mouth and the Serpent's Mouth, the old navigator thought that he had discovered the river that flowed out of the earthly paradise.

This we know to be the delusion of an old and ill man, yet in a way it is a symbol of the unknown world that Columbus had opened up. As we have seen in this book, excavations in thousands of jungle-covered mounds of Central and South America have revealed something Columbus never knew: that the bronze-skinned people of the Americas were the creators of some of the world's most beautiful art and architecture. The skills from which this wonderful and sometimes terrifying art flowed were almost crushed out when its creators were conquered by the white men. But, like a great river flowing underground, the sensitiveness and the passion of the artists lived on in the blood of their descendants, to rise again now in the art and music of Mexico and other countries south of our own.

By nature a contemplative and artistic people, the Indians will give to the future certain qualities developed during their thousands of years in the Americas. Future American art and culture will be enormously enriched by their art, which was born of the vast spaces and solitudes of the plains, the sun of the deserts, and the rich, quick-growing life of the jungles. All of these things were known to the ancestors of the Indians at a time when our own European ancestors were hunting the bison, the giant deer, and the mastodon with spears and traps, aided by torch-lit magic rites carried on deep in caves before the painted images of these animals.

The Americas should have been named after the man who had been christened Cristoforo Colombo. Instead, they took their name from a black-eyed, hook-nosed Florentine named Amerigo Vespucci, who, in a letter written to Lorenzo de' Medici in 1504, described his third voyage to the New World. This letter was printed as a pamphlet called the *Mundus Novus,* and became very popular.

Later, Martin Waldseemüller, engaged in mapping this great unknown country, reasoned that since Europe and Asia got their names from women, the New World should be named after a man, and on his map he put the name of the man whose popular little booklet he had admired.

So, most casually, the Americas were named. But on the tomb of Columbus in the Cathedral of Seville the true legend is engraved: "To Castile and León He Gave a New World."

Castile and León could not hold it: it was too big for them. What Columbus had done was to give a fresh New World to the Old World. He himself had fulfilled a prophecy made fourteen centuries earlier by Seneca, in lines which Columbus, perhaps with his fingers guided by a sense of destiny, had written in a copybook which he kept as a young man:

There will come a time when the ocean sea will disclose its secret and a sailor shall discover a new world, and then shall Thule be no longer the last of lands.

XIV: A DECADE OF DISCOVERY

In the ten years since this book was first published, archaeologists have learned many interesting new things about early man in the New World. Before we look at some of the new theories as to man's arrival here, let us pause to view some of those early comers who, according to Carbon-14 dating, are now thought to have been already at home in the continent before the last Ice Age blew its chilly breath down America's backbone.

LEWISVILLE MAN, CIRCA 42,000 B.C. While C-14 dating of his artifacts is not entirely agreed upon, new tests made by the Humble Oil Company date "Lewisville Man" back to 42,000 B.C. Although C-14 dating is not yet proof against error, we can safely consider Lewisville Man to be the earliest known Texan: Americanists are still havin , rather bad luck with fossils of early man. As you read on page ,, "Minnesota Man" (or Minnie) was found back in 1932, with · ʒxperts present to guarantee that she could defend her title oʰ ʒs Ice-Age America. Some two decades later Dr. Helmut de ʿ erra had the hard luck to be away from the site when his workers crashed through the layer above an ancient fossil man who bogged down near two stranded mammoths, in the valley of Mexico, perhaps 12,000 years ago.

Lewisville Man could, therefore, have made himself very popular with archaeologists by dying in some protected place where his bones might have become fossilized. Alas, however, Lewisville Man is purely a deduction: he is not a man at all but only a hammer stone, a flake scraper, a chopper and some twenty hearths with quantities of datable charcoal, found at Lewisville, Texas, in 1956. As if thrown in to make things harder, the researchers also found a single Clovis-type spear-point, a type which according to other C-14 and geological-strata dating was not made until some fifteen thousand years later. The Clovis-type point may have worked its way down into the Lewisville assembly line but the twenty-one hearths must have been constructed, filled, and fired by man. Lewisville cooks burned wood so lavishly that the Humble Oil Company has a stockpile of charcoal for testing as C-14 methods are refined.

Other evidence confirms this early date. Some fifty types of animal bones, including those of mammoth and camel, were found with the hearths. The larger animals are represented only by disjointed pieces, as if the Lewisville people had hacked limbs off the leavings of some more powerful carnivore, perhaps Smilodon the saber-tooth himself.

Though Lewisville man was not found, as early as 1940 a skull had been unearthed in a sandpit some twenty-five miles away, in the same Upper Shuler geological formation. Chemical tests date this skull back to only about 13,000 B.C., however, so he could have been only a remote descendant of Lewisville people. Even so, the eyes in this ancient brain-case must have looked out upon America long before the last ice advance.

SANTA ROSA MAN AND THE DWARF MAMMOTH, CIRCA 27,650 B.C. The most baffling of the new discoveries is that of men who for an estimated thirteen thousand years feasted on dwarf mammoth, whose remains are found only on Santa Rosa Island, now some forty miles off the coast of California. While truly mammoth mammoths roamed the Americas, Santa Rosa was cut off from the California mainland by sinking land or rising seas, perhaps a million years ago. As often happens to species in a limited environment, the stranded mammoths dwindled to an island-sized variety, only four to six feet tall and perhaps not as wary as might have been desirable, for somehow, sometime, man came to prey on them.

We may be sure that fire-bearing man was not stranded with the mammoth on Santa Rosa a million years ago. Either Santa

Rosa became an island later than geologists now think or else man arrived there by one of several ways, each more improbable than the last.

During the Wisconsin glaciation, because enormous quantities of sea water were on cold storage in glaciers, sea levels were lowered to such an extent that Santa Rosa may have been only two miles offshore. There is still little reason to imagine that any human couple voluntarily waded farther into the icy Pacific than was necessary to pick up their daily sea food. The use of boats made of rushes for early American coastwise trips has recently been suggested. Or perhaps Santa Rosa pioneers were swept to sea on a flood-uprooted tree; many Pacific islands have received small animals on such natural rafts. If the island had touched the mainland again, the dwarf mammoth would surely have disembarked and might have left his bones somewhere about, perhaps in the La Brea tar pit, but none such have been found.

Louis Brennan suggests in *No Stone Unturned* that man may have arrived on Santa Rosa from the seaward side, via land connections now undersea. Oceanographers may have to come to the aid of archaeologists before this and other unsolved questions can be settled: there is much to learn yet about Easter Island, about many cultural traits curiously similar to those found in Peru and in Polynesia, and about art motifs which are very alike in Southeastern Asia and Middle America.

The International Geophysical Year (I.G.Y.) has brought forth evidence that the Pacific ocean floor heaves and buckles like an indignant bronco, though in somewhat slower motion, and the Atlantic is hardly more pacific, if one may pun on so vast a subject. Either of them is perfectly capable of heaving up land bridges, given some forty thousand years in which to do it. Whatever happened at Santa Rosa, the time came when Santa Rosa man found his bridges sunk behind him and settled down to carve dwarf mammoth steaks with unshaped flint chips. Human bones have been discovered in the same location as charcoal dated at about 11,000 B.C., which represents a respectable antiquity. But life must have been easy on Santa Rosa, since man unimaginatively used these same tools for thousands of years after his contemporaries over on the mainland and in Eurasia were making improved ones of chipped flint.

However man arrived, C-14 datings on three samples of Santa Rosa charcoal, probably of human origin, average 27,650 B.C., plus or minus twenty-five hundred years. Almost the whole of Egyptian history could be packed into this plus-minus margin for error, but time probably marched on more productively in historical Egypt than it did on Santa Rosa. The weather, however, was doing a remarkable amount of changing, shifting from cold to warm and back again as minor glacial advances and retreats took place. Over on the mainland, men were having to find new ways of earning their daily food.

"TULE SPRINGS MAN," CIRCA 21,800 B.C. Before Nevada became a semi-desert, however, hunters camped by a stream there, made fires, and cut up game with simple chip tools rather like those Santa Rosa man used. They strewed the camp site untidily with bones of camel, horse, deer, and mammoth. These remains are those of immature and enfeebled animals, which most often fall prey to unskilled hunters. The camp site, six hundred feet long and two hundred feet wide, was large enough to allow a number of things to be lost there. These included chipped and pointed tools, a biface (worked on both sides) chopper, two scrapers, and two biface discoidal objects of unknown use, resembling chipped stone disks found in early European sites. Not present there, the researchers noted, were projectile points or metates (scooped-out rocks, in which seeds were crushed by means of a round stone called a mano). Since manos are usually found in the sites of seed-grinding people, their absence at Tule Springs adds to the picture of this camp as that of primitive hunters. Tule

Springs charcoal has been C-14 dated as earlier than 21,800 B.C., the sample being too small for more accurate dating.

AMERICAN PEBBLE TOOLS? Were the Santa Rosa, the Lewisville, and the Tule Springs people America's earliest tool-makers? There is evidence to suggest that they were not. Amerinds are thought by several students to have made pebble-tools like those found by Dr. and Mrs. L. S. B. Leakey in Olduvai Gorge, Tanganyika. Alas, America has no Olduvai Gorge, where the evidences of a half million years of occupation are stacked away almost as neatly as cards in a filing system. To make things more difficult for hard-working archaeologists, the early American hunters seem to have preferred open-air sites to caves.

Finding such an ancient camp site, with its thin layer of debris, is difficult unless natural events, such as floods and erosion, cut down to expose it, or unless the site is near a spring or lake where people lived for longer periods, and whose ancient borders may be traced out by geologists. Unlike caves, open sites are subject to severe wind and water erosion. Debris tends to scatter away. Winds and floods deposit layers of earth above the camp site with its handful of chipped stones and its few burned rocks, which to the untrained eye are all "just rocks." Only a sealed-away hidden site will retain the charcoal, bone, shell, and other materials helpful for C-14 dating.

THE LEHNER-NACO ELEPHANT KILLS, CIRCA 11,000 B.C. Erosion may quickly ruin the ancient camp and butchering sites it exposes. American archaeology, therefore, is greatly indebted to Edward F. Lehner for his prompt reporting to Arizona University of bones exposed in an arroyo bank in Cochise county, in southeastern Arizona. Here experts excavated the remains of nine immature mammoths and those of horse, bison, and tapirs, along with thirteen projectile points, eight butchering tools, and charcoal from two fires. The tools included scrapers, a knife, and a chopper. Microscopic analysis indicates that the stone was local in origin.

Ernst Antevs reports that the geological evidence suggests a rather moist, sub-arid climate, preceding the Datin drought which he thinks eliminated most of the American elephants some ten thousand years ago. The report made by Emil W. Haury, Ernst Antevs, and other experts in the July 1959 issue of *American Antiquity* is an exciting account of a rare discovery, handled with painstaking archaeological methods.

The Lehner and the Naco sites twelve miles away mark the southwesternmost point where Llano man is now known to have hunted big game with his fluted Clovis points. Antevs gave a geological dating of thirteen thousand years for these bones and artifacts, which is supported by the C-14 dating of charcoal at around 12,000 B.C. The Cochise food-collecting culture of Sulphur Springs came along somewhat later. A slow transition from big-game herd hunting to food collecting may have taken place here, even before the large Pleistocene animals became extinct. The difference between the two ways of living may not have been as sharp as was once thought.

Thus the accumulation of the evidence about America's earliest tool-makers has been difficult and slow. Nonetheless, by haunting glacier moraines, bulldozer tracks, eroding cliffs, and abandoned gravel pits, as well as by digging in likely locations, archaeologists have found a number of stone tools which look remarkably like those used by early man in Africa and Eurasia. Hand-sized pebbles chipped on one edge have been found all over the Americas, though they were usually not recognized as hand-axes.

In 1956 Miss Freddie Curtiss took some forty-seven such stones from the Archaeological Survey Association's collections to show to European experts in stone-age tools, who found among them some that looked very like the pebble tools used some three hundred thousand years ago by Eurasian early men called Clactonian and Abbevillean, from the sites in England and France where their industries were first described.

Meanwhile, E. B. Renaud, trained by Europe's great Paleolithic expert, the Abbé Breuil, collected over two thousand such pieces from five hundred sites in four Western states. Renaud himself compared many of these with Clactonian tools but did not claim any such age for the American tools, saying instead, "It seems, therefore, much more reasonable to consider the Clactonian merely as an early and relatively simple technique of manufacturing flakes and flake implements by the hand-hammer method." Indeed, nothing could be more reasonable if you once assume that tool-making creatures will find similar solutions for similar problems, given such materials as stone, bone, wood, shell, and horn to work with. The problems involved in early man's life were remarkably similar wherever he found himself: i.e., how to kill an animal, skin off its hide, cut up the meat, and cure the hide for use as clothing or shelter, if the climate made shelter and clothing necessary, as happened where the glaciers spread.

The hunt for the earliest American tools has had interesting results in South America. Julius Spinner of Chile read a paper at the Paris 1960 International Congress of Anthropological and Ethnological Sciences, entitled, "Are There Any Neanderthal Men or Neanderthal Hybrids in South America?" Neanderthal man is usually considered the maker of the Paleolithic artifacts called Mousterian. Spinner lists various Mousterian-like tools found on the Pacific coast of South America, in the altiplano of South Bolivia, and in Chile. Spinner does not, however, believe with Renaud that this resemblance represents only a stage of independent tool-making.

Instead, he points to a considerable number of "very old osseous materials" (fossilized bones, to us) which display the Neanderthaloid-type brow-ridge, retreating forehead, and under-developed chin. Speculatively, Spinner traces these facial characteristics right down to representations on human-faced urns and figures found in the early agricultural phases of South America. He com-

pares these and other art motifs with similar ones from the early
agricultural cultures of the Ancient Near East. Pointing out that
we now know that Neanderthals and neo-men intermarried at
Mt. Carmel, he asks if a similar mixture may have arrived in the
New World. It is an intriguing thought.

The question of early man in the Americas will prove less difficult to work out when we know more about the extent of former
land areas, now under water, which were migration routes and
settlement areas when ocean levels were some three hundred
feet lower during ice advances. Kenneth W. Vinton has made
a study of his own area, Panama, even to the extent of having
skin-divers explore under-sea caves which were above water
within the time of man in America. Vinton delivered a paper at
the 1960 Americanists Congress in Vienna, called "Carbon-dated
Ocean Level Changes, Offering a New System of Correlating
Archaeological Date." Ocean levels were some seventy feet lower
when men were in this area some seven thousand years ago,
though the Panama picture is complicated by rising coasts. Dr.
Vinton's charts correlated human habitations with ocean-level
changes, a job which needs to be done in many other areas where
early men lived.

Remembering that sea levels were quite different even a few
thousand years ago, we need to re-study the problem of man's
migrations. The May 1960 issue of *Scientific American* had an
article by Dr. Rhodes W. Fairbridge, called "The Changing Level
of the Sea," which discusses the fact that when climates warmed,
glaciers melted promptly, and sea levels rose, often so disastrously
to man that flood legends are universally found. With our American hunters and their herds in mind, we may dwell upon Dr.
Fairbridge's picture of the fairly recent past:

Drowned beaches at the edge of the continental shelf show that
17,000 years ago, at the height of the last large-scale advance of the
glaciers, the world-wide sea level was some 330 feet lower than it is

today. As the great North American and Scandinavian glaciers melted, the sea level began to rise at a rate of about 40 inches per century. . . . The greatest and fastest rise yet discovered in the geological record reached its crest about 6000 years ago. The cumulative incursion of the sea flooded low-lying coastal lands in every part of the world. This was the deluge that drowned the homes and troubled the legends of the ancients.

This deluge also drowned the camp sites of the early Americans who lived all along the coasts of the Americas, including broad areas of Alaska and of the Caribbean which have been flooded out for the past six thousand years. We have only to study the shallow sea depths in the Caribbean area to see what a vast attractive homeland it would have presented to beast and man when glacial advances made more northern parts of America uncomfortable. We should not be surprised, then, that the early great civilizations of the Americas developed around this section, which archaeologists call Nuclear America. Here man had food in abundance, when damper times prevailed and when animal herds were still flourishing: here perhaps people were forced to live together as rising sea levels progressively wiped out their earlier homes, and were forced to find new ways of providing food as animals decreased and human populations increased. The development of maize was to provide the solution to this problem, a solution which brought with it the splendor of the Toltec and Maya civilizations.

THE ALASKA-CHUCKCHI PROVINCE. A second great area of the American pioneer's development centered in what is now the Bering Straits area. Bering is no longer considered as having been merely a bridge over which prehistoric Asian man hurried, clutching the spear he was importing into the New World. Instead, it is now known to have been a large province where men lived for thousands of years, moving about chiefly to take advantage of the best seasonal foods as berries ripened, fish spawned, and animals congregated. There was much more land at Bering some fifteen thousand years ago, when sea levels were 330 feet lower than today. David Hopkins of the United States Geological Survey estimated in 1959 that some thirty-five thousand years ago the Alaskan-Chuckchi province may have been a thousand miles wide, north to south—a very sizeable land-bridge indeed.

Not enough snow fell here to build glaciers, and thus people had time to learn how to adapt themselves to ice advances. Dr. J. L. Giddings and others who have excavated five-thousand-year-old sites of human occupation here see a great difference between the tools of these people and of Asians.

Dr. Giddings summed this up in the March 1960 issue of *Current Anthropology:*

The Bering Strait region is the traditional gateway to America. Theory has had weary migrants wearing paths across its dried-up floor in glacial times and, later, paddling primitive craft in a determined search for a new world. The archaeology of the region steadfastly refuses, however, to divulge the short-term sites of people on the move. It shows, rather, the slowly changing record of several groups of indigenous hunters and fishermen and their descendants, whose artifacts were specialized to a remarkable extent for the taking of food from the seas, streams, tundras, and forests, and whose interests were as local as the shores and river banks on which they dwelt. . . . We need not give up the search for evidence of the migration of small bands, or even of uneasy hordes; yet the emphasis can be, for a time, on the cultural stability of a Bering Strait which is a center, rather than a way-station, of circum-polar ideas.

BACK TO BERING? Alex Krieger had pointed out as early as 1952 that Clovis-Folsom hunters could hardly have brought their spear points from Asia via Siberia, since these points were used in the Southwest long before they appeared in Alaskan strata. Traffic may indeed have reversed itself as the Southwest dried out, and rolled back over Bering. The Clovis fluted-point people, instead of dying away to be replaced by another race of hunters who used the Folsom fluted points, may have followed the mammoth herds northward, the mammoths seeking their retreating pasturage and the hunters their retreating steaks.

Ultimately all may have arrived at the taiga-tundra cold front. Here hunters from the plains may have met caribou hunters of the taiga-tundra region, using the micro-liths whose delicacy may have fascinated the Clovis stone-smiths. If the taigans were as friendly as Eskimos are, and if the mammoth hunters did not try to take over the caribou herds, each might have learned from the other. Giddings says of the Denbigh flint complex of about 2900 B.C., "Some of the larger bifaced points closely resemble some from the early western American plains."

When mammoths died away and when the bison herds flourished in the Southwest, they were hunted with the dainty, fancy Folsom point rather than with the larger, plainer Clovis point. The taigans and the herd-hunters may have exchanged calling cards, given a large area and several thousand years to do it.

WHAT HAPPENED TO THE PLEISTOCENE ANIMALS? A decade's research has not yet solved this problem. Kenneth MacGowan gave us a vivid picture of the death of some of the mammoths, in *Early Man in the New World:*

They lie frozen in tangled masses, interspersed with uprooted trees. They seem to have been torn apart and dismembered and then consolidated under catastrophic conditions. Yuma and Plainview spear points and perhaps one generalized Folsom have been found in these chill beds. Skin, ligament, hair, flesh, can still be seen.

The mystery of the frozen mammoths is not yet solved. There is no indication that these mysterious Alaskan beds represented a death trap arranged by man. Perhaps something truly catastrophic happened to produce the tangled masses of mammoths that are described by MacGowan, but for the disappearance of the species itself a somewhat less catastrophic explanation must be found.

Louis Brennan, in *No Stone Unturned,* has advanced a reasonable one: that simple starvation destroyed the species, that as the bison multiplied they literally ate the food out from under the trunks of the mammoths, by over-cropping the pasturage. As mammoths disappeared, Brennan thinks, the great cats and dire wolves fell upon the horses and camels, and then, having eaten themselves out of hide and hoof, themselves starved away. The bison, Brennan conjectures, might have presented too massive a shoulder-phalanx even for Smilodon. (Having closely observed lion, elephant and buffalo in East Africa, and having been far more afraid of the buffalo than of anything else, this writer agrees that any predator must think twice before attacking buffalo. But having seen herds of zebras and wildebeest—gnu to you—grazing peacefully away and then sailing off just as the baffled lioness sprang, she finds it impossible to believe that carnivores destroyed the vast herds of American horses and camels. Either some great climate shift or some pandemic disease must also be taken into the picture of the disappearing Pleistocene herds, along with the devastations of man the hunter.)

TIME AND CHANGE. During his forty-thousand-plus years in the Americas, the Amerind rolled up an impressive record of inventiveness. Several different ways of living had developed as early as 15,000 B.C. We have already looked at the way of the herd-hunters, whose great game reservation swept from Alaska to the Mexican highlands and along the South American pampas. Outside this game area, even during the time of the great herds, there were many other people, leading less spectacular lives in desert or wooded areas. These people knew how to use whatever the land afforded: grains, seed, acorns, nuts, fruits, game, snakes, gophers, fish, turtles, turkeys and other birds, shellfish, and so on.

People who live like this are called usufructians (from *usus,* use, and *fructus,* fruit), and there were a great many of them by 10,000 B.C., even before their ranks were swelled by the luckless hunters of vanishing herds.

In addition to these two ways of living which have existed from time immemorial (man's primate ancestors were usufructians, as were the tree shrews which were in the lower branches of the family tree) there was a variation which was already well developed five thousand years ago. This was the way of life found then, and now, in the circum-polar zone. Here people had slowly adjusted as the Ice Ages forced them to do so, to live in the taiga, the northernmost woods, on the tundra, the treeless Arctic plain, and even along the chilly Arctic Sea's icy fringe. The people living in this most desperately difficult zone have, surprisingly enough, changed least.

The life of the hunters was necessarily determined by the life of the herds. As mammoths traveled north during a retreating glacial time, the Clovis people followed, not only north toward Bering but also east. Clovis points are found all across the Atlantic seaboard, at seemingly successively later dates. Those at Bull Brook, Massachusetts, have been given a C-14 dating of 7000 B.C. As time and distance widened between these wanderers and their earlier happier hunting ground, their projectile points changed. At Graham Cave, Missouri, the last fluted points appear along with usufructian artifacts, as if the herdless hunters had settled down to the duller life of collecting. Had this occurred only at Graham Cave we might think that we were dealing with some prehistoric collector's treasure trove, for why should we assume that only modern men like to find and keep dainty chipped stone points? But it happens frequently. One can hardly avoid the conclusion that man the hunter refused to die away with his herds but, doubtless with a sigh about the good old days, settled down to take lesser game.

FROM SEED-GATHERERS TO AGRICULTURALISTS? Though to a greater extent than was once realized the Amerind had been keeping pace with his contemporaries in other continents, he fell behind at this stage, during which in the ancient Middle Eastern men were domesticating animals and plants, learning the use of metals, and developing urban centers. The Amerind did not lack inventiveness. He undoubtedly was somewhat out of the range of easy spread of ideas from the Middle East. Yet early Americans ground seeds into meal almost as early as this happened in other places. In his book *Danger Cave* Jesse B. Jennings lists objects used in Utah before 7000 B.C., and it is an impressive list: percussion chipped tools, the atlatl or spear thrower, a fire drill (a tool for making fire by spinning a rod of wood on a base of wood), woven sandals, knotted nets, and rabbit-hair fur cloth, along with other things. Jennings dates twined basketry here to 7000 B.C., even arguing that basketry and weaving were practiced in North America "before textile work was known in the Eurasiatic neolithic." He points out that the harvesting and milling of small grains was known over the Desert area by 8000 B.C., which compares favorably with the Middle East date.

Jennings believes that the people of these caves he so carefully studied (Danger, Raven, and—believe it or not—Juke Box) may have invented their own bows and arrows. Asiatics were long given credit for this invention, which appeared in Western Europe only during the Mesolithic, some ten thousand years ago. The large American stone projectile points were once thought to have been used only on spears. Oren F. Evans of the University of Oklahoma tried out some of them as arrow heads and came to the surprising conclusion that until people learned to put feathers on their shafts the points used on arrows would have had to be big. New large shapes appeared some four thousand years ago and may represent some change in shooting technique. As early as 2000 B.C. the Danger Cave people used shafts with quills.

GRAHAM CAVE, MISSOURI, CIRCA 7700 B.C. The great advantage of caves, to archaeologists, is that they provide datable layers which show a slow change in man's way of living. The lowest layers of Graham Cave have been given a C-14 dating of 7700 B.C., and contain the familiar group of choppers, scrapers, and atlatls. Following this clear signature of the hunters comes that of seed-grinders, who used pestles, mortars, and manos, and decorated themselves with a variety of pins, beads, and paints. Early pottery also appears. Groups of stone balls found together suggest the use of the bola, still employed by Argentine cowboys to throw cattle by entangling their legs with leather thongs attached to stones.

RUSSELL CAVE, ALABAMA, CIRCA 7700 B.C. In Russell Cave the projectile points, atlatls, baskets, and the full line of stone tools are also followed in due time by the grain-grinder's tools. Here a stone pestle was buried beside its probable owner, a forty-five-year-old man who was only five feet two inches tall. The most surprising find at Russell Cave, however, was not its inhabitant but a hinged fish hook, and an animal-fat wick lamp made from a bear's foreleg hollowed out and packed with fat. Both were found in an eight-thousand-year-old layer. Time was marching on; the Amerind had his lamp to read his newspaper by, though his newspaper was still the tracks on the forest floor. These artifacts are like those used much later by Eskimos and other circum-polar people, explain it how you will. Snug under their skin shelters to protect them from drips in the cave roofs, and with their lamps near at hand, these people enjoyed a diet which included fish, turkeys, nuts, grains, deer, fruits, salads and other delicacies reminding us of our Thanksgiving Day, itself an Amerind harvest festival which the Puritans learned from Indians who helped them survive.

Not everyone could live in caves. Even those who could probably sent out parties who made camps while locating the season's food offerings. Dr. J. L. Coe of the University of North Carolina has located in the Carolina piedmont a series of small sites where projectile point forms are found which resemble those in Russell Cave. Were these sites outlying camps for those who went to gather seasonal food supplies? Or were they the homes of small family bands who had left more crowded locations?

The Amerinds of those days had more to be thankful for than they could have realized, even aside from the fact that the white conquerors were still thousands of years in the future. The period from 7000 to 4500 B.C. was favorable from the standpoint of climate—no longer too cold and wet and not yet too hot. The "Anathermal" ("return of warmth," as Ernst Antevs, glaciologist and geologist, named it) was like the Little Bear's porridge, neither too hot nor too cold. The following "Altithermal," which caused the Southwest to dry to the famine point, only pleasantly warmed the rivers and hills of the Eastern forests, causing the range of shellfish to extend northward. This gave the east-coast people a chance to settle down in larger groups and happily pile up shellfish refuse mounds or middens. Sea levels were lower then, and many of these middens are doubtless now beneath the waves, but enough remain to show that the East-erners were steadily if slowly improving their fish hooks, cutting wood and using it for dugout canoes, grinding flour of acorns and grains, and making pottery. The subject of pottery is a specialist's area: one can say here only that a number of papers presented at the two anthropological congresses in Europe in the summer of 1960 were devoted to the probably independent origin and devel-opment of Amerind pottery in various American areas.

The Altithermal warmth was broken by another advance of the ice, the Cochrane, which improved life for people in the Southwest until the return of the warmth. All and all, it had been a busy and upsetting several thousand years. The usufructians of the central Mississippi area came out of it rather well, and were soon on their way to the developments which, before the time of

Christ, flowered into the Mound Builder culture. Down in Nuclear America even more spectacular advances toward civilization had taken place, which we cannot attempt to retrace here.

The usufructians, who could "live off the land" almost anywhere, had long since adapted themselves to every kind of living condition in America. We need not picture them as striking boldly for the unknown. Rather, they must have spread slowly as family groups increased and young sons moved with their own families to the nearest undefended or capturable territory, continuing to get together with "the folks" for special occasions.

We may be sure that these occasions were gay and spectacular. They may have occurred when berries, nuts, acorns, fish, or game were especially plentiful, or after the wild grasses, nuts, acorns, and other harvests were safely stored away in clay-lined baskets or pots. Family bonds were strengthened and new alliances made. Older people retold ancient tales and tribal lore, while younger ones tested their skills and made new friends. Mothers and wives undoubtedly studied each other's baskets, textiles, pearl or copper ornaments, or combinations for the cooking pot. Here were the beginnings of confederations, which were to reach such remarkable developments of statesmanship and oratory in the Eastern forests. Here were the shamans, the custodians of dance and song and pantomime, bedecked in their most impressive rattles and feathers and paints.

These early American medicine men were the forerunners not only of the doctors and the surgeons but also of the priests and prophets, the artists and the musicians, the astronomers and the architects who were to build the great Middle American cultures of later days. They developed a wide range of herbal remedies and poisons. They discovered and used vision-giving cacti and mushrooms. They found game and missing objects by methods we would today label as psychic, and interpreted dreams and visions quite as cleverly as our psychoanalysts do. They foretold the future by a variety of methods, often doubtless with a considerable degree of accuracy, for this skill was found to be highly developed among the Amerinds of Central America at the time of the discovery of America.

The shaman was also the teacher of the young, training them by means of elaborate rituals involving very long chants which had to be letter-perfect. The shamans' skill in surgery is attested by evidences of bone-setting and amputation, as well as by numerous skulls showing trepanning operations considered delicate even today. The medicine doctors of later days, as we know from post-discovery records, cured many illnesses which we would today diagnose as psychosomatic, and refused to treat others which they knew to be beyond the power of suggestion or herbal remedies. Naturally they had some tricks up their sleeves, to maintain prestige when neither their skill nor their psychic powers could be relied upon. They studied the stars, the courses of the planets across the skies, and the phases of the moon. This knowledge, which extended even to the phases of the planet Venus, flowered in the calendar systems used among the Mayas, the Toltecs, and the Aztecs.

DOMESTICATION. It is likely that we must hand the palm to the usufructians for most of this development, and without doubt they were the ones who domesticated plants. It is likely that the two ways of living—the nomadism of herd hunting and the more limited wandering of the usufructians—flowed together after the disappearance of the Pleistocene herds. Down in Nuclear America plant domestication, as you may see by studying the chart on page 14, began as early as 5000 B.C., with the cultivation of squash and probably of pepper, gourds, and small beans. The use of beans, a high-energy protein food which can serve well as a meat substitute, spread rather widely after 3000 B.C. Meanwhile, the breeding of maize out of wild corn was under way, and by 3500 B.C. corn cobs appear among Cochise remains in the Southwest.

The whole process of the development of the American Indians' culture is summarized by Dr. Gordon Willey in the January 8, 1960, issue of *Science*. Doctor Willey makes the point that plant domestication was an affair of local plants until the development of the high-energy crop, maize, made the growth of villages and urban centers possible. Along with the spread of maize the greater development of crafts and ultimately of arts became possible. Cotton was in use by 2000 B.C. or earlier, as is shown at Huaca Prieta. Manioc and yams were cultivated in lowland Venezuela by 1000 B.C. or earlier. At this same date, sunflowers and pumpkins were raised by the Adena Mound Builders. While evidence for maize as the basis of this great flowering of culture is still lacking, Willey and others feel that such a development could hardly have taken place without the support of a reliable food crop.

Why did this development from hunting and gathering to food production and urban centers take place almost five thousand years later in the Americas than in the Old World, when earlier Amerinds seem to have been well abreast of Old World developments? Doctor Willey suggests that until the development of maize the Amerinds may have lacked a food supply which could compete with the oats, wheat, and barley of the Old World.

It is also true that the Amerinds failed to domesticate animals, which were so important a part of the cultures developing in the Old World. The great herds of horses and large camels had died away in the Americas around 9000 B.C., leaving only the small camel relatives in the Andes, which were duly domesticated by the Andean people. But why did the Amerinds not domesticate bison, wild pigs, mountain goats, and other possible sources of food? Why did they raise turkeys for their feathers but not on a large scale for food? Louis Brennan reminds us that the Indians prayed to the gods of life, asking pardon that life must be taken for his food. Perhaps to enslave an animal would have required a change in the Amerind belief that nature is a web of life in which all living things are related to one another.

In this short summary of the last decade's discoveries, we cannot include the enormous work done on the higher cultures. C-14 dates the Mound Builder cultures back far earlier than was once supposed: a date of 336 B.C. has been given to the Havana Mound group in Illinois, an Adema mound in Ohio is dated at 780 B.C., and an early Hopewell group in New York State at 800 B.C. This is the most abrupt reversal which C-14 dating has brought in the decade of its use.

Much more is now known about the urban centers, such as the capital of the Chimu, the city Chanchan, on the Peruvian coast, which was destroyed by the Incas in 1470 A.D. The great cultures of the Mayas, Toltecs, Aztecs, and Incas have been studied in detail by a number of careful scholars and their magnificent achievements loom up even more impressively than before.

Unfortunately little of the great Amerind heritage exists in written form. Much has been permitted to be lost of the oral tradition which still remained only a few years ago. There is no doubt however that a great poetry and philosophy, as well as a marvelous architecture and art, were developed in America. The Indian moral virtues were also great ones.

The wisest sages of the rest of the world have never improved upon the Golden Rule of the Shawnees:

Do not kill or injure your neighbor, for it is not he that you injure; you injure yourself. But do good to him, therefore add to his days of happiness as you add to your own.

Do not wrong or hate your neighbor, for it is not he that you wrong; you wrong yourself. But love him, for Manitou loves him also as he loves you.

SUGGESTED READINGS

*Brennan, Louis A. *No Stone Unturned*. Random House, 1959.

Douglas, Frederic H., and d'Harnoncourt, René. *Indian Arts of the United States*. Museum of Modern Art, 1941.

Embree, Edwin Rogers. *Indians of the Americas; Historical Pageant*. Houghton Mifflin, 1939.

Grant, Bruce. *American Indians: Yesterday and Today*. Dutton, 1958.

*Griffin, James, ed. *Archeology of Eastern United States*. University of Chicago Press, 1952.

Hibben, Frank C. *The Lost Americans*. Crowell, 1946.

*MacGowan, Kenneth. *Early Man in the New World*. Macmillan, 1950.

Marriott, Alice. *The First Comers*. Longmans, 1960.

Mason, Bernard S. *Book of Indian Crafts and Costumes*. Ronald Press, 1946.

Mead, Margaret. *People and Places*. World, 1959.

Morris, Ann Axtell. *Digging in Yucatan*. Doubleday, 1931.

Peck, Anne Merriman. *Pageant of Middle American History*. Longmans, 1947.

Shippen, Katherine B. *New Found World*. Viking, 1945.

Stefansson, Evelyn. *Here Is Alaska*. (Rev. ed.) Scribner, 1959. *Within the Circle*. Scribner, 1945.

Stirling, Matthew, et al., eds. *National Geographic Society on Indians of the Americas*. National Geographic Society, 1958.

*Underhill, Ruth. *Red Man's America*. University of Chicago Press, 1953.

Verrill, A. Hyatt, and Verrill, Ruth. *America's Ancient Civilizations*. Putnam, 1953.

*Wormington, H. M. *Ancient Man in North America*. Denver Museum of Natural History, 1957.

* An asterisk indicates titles of standard books for mature readers.

PAPERBOUND BOOKS

Many excellent books on anthropology are available in inexpensive paperbound editions. The following are suggested as examples of good background for mature readers.

Benedict, Ruth. *Patterns of Culture*. New American Library.

Childe, Gordon. *Man Makes Himself*. New American Library.

Firth, Raymond. *Human Types*. New American Library.

Huntington, Ellsworth. *Mainsprings of Civilization*. New American Library.

Montague, Ashley. *Man, His First Million Years*. New American Library.

Mason, V. Alden. *The Ancient Civilization of Peru*. Penguin.

Vaillant, G. C. *The Aztecs of Mexico*. Penguin.

GLOSSARY

Artifact. A product of human workmanship; one of the simpler products of primitive art, as distinguished from a natural object.

Atlatl. A throwing stick; a stick used by ancient Mexicans for throwing a spear.

Calmecac. Aztec school for priests.

Calpulli. Among the Aztecs, the fundamental unit of society.

Cenote. A natural underground water reservoir.

Conquistador. A leader in the Spanish conquest of America, especially of Mexico and Peru, in the 16th century.

Estufa (Sp., a stove). An assembly room in a Pueblo Indian dwelling; a kiva.

Fair God. Variously identified with Quetzalcoatl, Kukulcan, and Viracocha. He was represented as white and bearded. According to legend, he sailed away to the east, promising to return. Cortés, upon landing, was mistaken for the returning god, and the advance of his army was thereby made easier.

Glyph. A carved figure or character, incised or in relief.

Gorget. A collar or neck ornament. A piece of armor defending the throat.

Hieroglyph. Any character the meaning of which is not obvious.

Huitzilopochtli. The Aztec War God.

Ice age. The glacial epoch.

Incensario (Sp., a censer). A vessel in which incense is burned.

Kayak. An Eskimo decked canoe, usually made of sealskin. The covering is laced around the paddler.

Kiva. In Pueblo Indian architecture, a ceremonial chamber, originally round and mainly underground.

Kukulcan. The plumed or feathered serpent, Creator God of the Mayas. Identified with Quetzalcoatl.

Maguey. The Mexican *agave;* the century plant.

Matriarchy. A social system in which all descent is traced in the female line, all children belonging to the mother's clan. Land, houses, and social position are sometimes inherited in the female line.

Mesa (Sp., a table). A natural terrace or flat-topped hill with abrupt or steeply sloping sides, common in the Southwest.

Neolithic or New Stone Age. An era starting about 10,000 b.c. and lasting some 7,000 years. It was notable for such advances as stone polishing, pottery making, use of bow and arrow, domestication of animals, cultivation of grain, and invention of the wheel. In Europe, it marked the beginning of settled village life.

Obsidian. A compact volcanic glass, usually black or very dark-colored.

Pachacamac. The principal god of the Chimus, later identified by the Incas with Viracocha. There was also a pre-Incaic religious center by this name.

Pleistocene era. The glacial epoch. In the Americas, Canada and northern and northeastern U. S. were largely covered with ice.

Plumed Serpent god. See Kukulcan.

Pueblo (Sp., a village). An Indian village of the Southwest, built of stone or adobe in the form of communal houses, sometimes of several stories or terraces.

Quetzal. A Central American bird with a magnificent tail. It was especially associated with the worship of Quetzalcoatl.

Quetzalcoatl. An Aztec god worshiped as the inventor and patron of arts and crafts and the author of Mexican civilization. He is identical with the Mayan Kukulcan.

Quipu. A contrivance used by the ancient Peruvians for arithmetical purposes and as a memory device. From a main cord hung smaller cords of different colors and meanings; knots placed in these represented definite numbers.

Saga. A story, historical or legendary or both, of Icelandic heroes.

Skald. An ancient Scandinavian poet who composed poems in honor of distinguished men and their achievements, and recited or sang them on public occasions. Equivalent to the Briton or Celtic bards.

Skraeling. In accounts of early Norse visits to America, the word used for an American Indian or Eskimo.

Stela (plu. stelae). A slab or pillar bearing an inscription; a pillarlike monument.

Teocentli (Sp., teosinte). A large annual grass of Mexico and Central America closely related to corn in appearance and growth habits.

Theocracy. Government or political rule by priests or clergy as representatives of God.

Thule. A name given by the ancients to the northernmost part of the habitable world. It has been variously identified as Norway, Iceland, or one of the Shetland Islands.

Tipi (tepee). An American Indian conical tent used by most of the Plains tribes.

Tlaloc. Aztec god of rain and thunder.

Tlazolteotl. Aztec goddess; the Earth Mother.

Totem pole. A pole or pillar, usually carved and painted, set up before certain houses of Indian tribes of northwest America.

Viracocha. The Creator God of the Incas. He has been identified with the Aztec Quetzalcoatl.

Xipe-totec. The Aztec god of sowing. Human victims sacrificed to him were flayed.

Xiuhtecutli, "The Old Old God." The Aztec fire god.

ACKNOWLEDGMENTS

The author acknowledges her indebtedness to a great number of people for their generous help and cooperation in the preparation of this book.

She records here her profound appreciation of the unfailing sympathy, encouragement, and practical help of Dr. John Gillin, Professor of Anthropology, University of North Carolina, and offers her hearty thanks.

To the following, for expert guidance in selecting and authenticating relevant anthropological material, her thanks are due and herewith gratefully given: To Dr. Herbert J. Spinden, Curator of Primitive and New World Culture, the Brooklyn Museum; to Mr. Frank M. Setzler, Head Curator of the Department of Anthropology of the United States National Museum; to Dr. Guy Benton Johnson, Professor of Sociology and Anthropology, University of North Carolina; to Dr. Carson Ryan, Kenan Professor of Education, University of North Carolina; and to Dr. Harry Tschopik, Jr., Assistant Curator of Ethnology, the American Museum of Natural History.

The author expresses her warm appreciation of the kindness shown her by Dr. James Bell Bullitt and Dr. James Osler Bailey, in helping with advice and criticism to improve the literary qualities of the book.

To Señora Mario Quiros particular thanks are due for expert assistance in typing the manuscript, and to Miss Amelia Munson of the Teachers' Library of the New York Public Library for valuable help in extending the scope and usefulness of the list of suggested readings. To all those others, too many to name individually, whose good counsel and friendly support have been immeasurably valued, the author here records her deep indebtedness and gives her hearty thanks.

To various individuals and organizations who have permitted the use of specific materials, grateful acknowledgment is made as follows:

To Dr. Frank Hibben, for permission to use his report of archeological proceedings as the basis for the account of the "Pueblo Art Gallery," Chapter V.

To Dr. Herbert J. Spinden for his kindness in permitting the reproduction of a photograph of his Maya Astronomer. Photograph: courtesy of the Brooklyn Museum.

To Dr. Pál Kelemen for the use of two photographs (Hieroglyphic Stairway, Copán, Honduras, and Inner Court of a Palace, Mitla, Mexico) from his book, *Medieval American Art* (New York: Macmillan, 1943).

To Mr. Harold S. Gladwin for courtesy in supplying a photograph of the Hohokam Bowl, from the collection of the Gila Pueblo, Arizona.

To the American Museum of Natural History for its generosity in permitting the use of photographs of the following: Spirit Mask, Alaska; Kachinas of the Hopi Indians, Arizona; Limestone Figure, Maize God, Copán, Honduras; Seated Clay Figure, Central Veracruz; Prehistoric Cliff Dwellings, Mesa Verde, Colorado; Model of Ruins, Copán, Honduras; Pyramid of the Sun, Teotihuacán, Mexico; Temple Base, Xochicalco, Mexico; Palace of the Nuns, Uxmal, Mexico; Maya Temple, model, Campeche, Mexico; Manchu Picchu, Peru; Stone Pipe, Human Effigy, Adena Mound, Ohio.

To the University of Tennessee for courtesy in permitting the use of a photograph of a Painted Stone Effigy, Lebanon, Tennessee. Photograph: courtesy of the Museum of Modern Art.

To the Denver Art Museum for courtesy in permitting the use of a photograph of a War Club, Iroquois, Pennsylvania. Photograph: courtesy of the Museum of Modern Art.

To the Indian Arts and Crafts Board, United States Department of the Interior, for courtesy in permitting the use of a photograph of an Awatovi Mural Painting, northeastern Arizona. Photograph: courtesy of the Museum of Modern Art.

To the following for courtesy in permitting the use of photographs:

The Peabody Museum, Harvard University: Mimbres Bowl, Mimbres Valley, New Mexico; a Mochica Portrait Vessel, Chicamac Valley, Peru; and "Rio Bec B," Quintana Roo, Mexico.

The University Museum, Philadelphia: a Deer Masquette, Key Marco, Florida; a Portrait Vessel, Early Chimu; a Gold Female Figure, Quimbaya Culture, Colombia; and Stone Walls, Cuzco, Peru.

The Carnegie Institution of Washington: a Temple Base, Uaxactún, Guatemala; the Temple of the Frescoes, Tulum, Mexico; the Temple of the Three Lintels, Chichen Itzá, Mexico; and Observatory or Caracol, Chichen Itzá, Mexico.

The Brooklyn Museum: the Temple of the Cross (model), Palenque, Mexico, and the Temple of the Frescoes (model), Tulum, Mexico.

The Santa Fe Railway: Pueblo Bonito, Chaco Canyon, New Mexico, and Taos Pueblo, New Mexico.

The Museum of Fine Arts, Boston: a Gold Staff Head, Colombia.

Pan American World Airways: the Temple of Quetzalcoatl, Teotihuacán, Mexico; detail of the Temple of Quetzalcoatl; and El Castillo, Chichen Itzá, Mexico.

The Museum of Modern Art: Pictograph of the Basketmaker Culture, Barrier Canyon, Utah.

The Museum of the American Indian, Heye Foundation, New York: Iroquois Cornhusk Mask. Photograph: courtesy of the Museum of Modern Art.

For the use of poems, acknowledgment is made as follows:

"Carib Song," p. 50, reprinted by courtesy of the American Folklore Society from an article entitled "Popular Notions Pertaining to Primitive Stone Artifacts in Surinam," *Journal of American Folklore*, Vol. 30 (1917), p. 259.

"With Dangling Hands," p. 61, "That Buffalo May Come," p. 82, "Song of the Sky Loom," p. 94, "From a Mayan Lament Against the Spanish Conquerors," p. 183, all from *Songs of the Tewa*, translated by Herbert J. Spinden, Exposition of Indian Tribal Arts, Inc., 1933. Reprinted by courtesy of Dr. Spinden.

"Hymn to Viracocha," p. 209, translated from the Spanish by Herbert J. Spinden, with reference to translations by Clements Robert Markham and Philip Ainsworth Means. Reprinted by courtesy of Dr. Spinden.

"Warrior Song of the Hethu'shka Society," p. 75, from *The Omaha Tribe* by Alice C. Fletcher and Francis La Flesche. Extract from the 27th Annual Report of American Ethnology. Washington: 1911. Reprinted by courtesy of the Smithsonian Institution, Bureau of American Ethnology.

"Iroquois Dirge," p. 118, from the *Iroquois Book of Rites*, edited by Horatio E. Hale. Philadelphia: D. G. Brinton, 1883.

"To the Lynx," p. 135, from *The Osage Tribe: Rite of the Wa-xo'-Be*, by Francis La Flesche. Bureau of American Ethnology, 45th Annual Report, 1927-28. Washington: Government Printing Office, 1930. Reprinted by courtesy of the Smithsonian Institution, Bureau of American Ethnology.

"Song of the Three Sisters" ("Hail! Hail! Hail! Thou who hast created all things"), p. 142, from *Story of the American Indian* by Paul Radin. New York: Liveright Publishing Corporation, 1944. Reprinted by courtesy of the Liveright Publishing Corporation.

"One Woman Paying Her Respects to Another," p. 144, translation by William Thalbitzer from *The Ammassalik Eskimo*, Part II, No. 3, Language and Folklore, Copenhagen, 1923. Reprinted by courtesy of Dr. Thalbitzer.

"Song of Cwatc," p. 144, from *Tlingit Myths and Legends*, by John R. Swanton. Bureau of American Ethnology Bulletin No. 39. Washington: Government Printing Office, 1909. Reprinted by courtesy of the Smithsonian Institution, Bureau of American Ethnology.

"Thorhall's Song on Leaving America," p. 111, from *Narratives of the Discovery of America,* edited by Arnold W. Lawrence and Jean Young. New York: Jonathan Cape and Harrison Smith, 1931.

"Mayan Prophetic Chant," p. 156, from *Essays of an Americanist* by Daniel G. Brinton. Philadelphia: Porter and Coates, 1890.

"A Song by Nezahualcoyotl," p. 184, from *Ancient Nahuatal Poetry* by Daniel G. Brinton. Library of American Aboriginal Literature, Philadelphia, 1887.

The author acknowledges the expert help and counsel given by a number of people in the preparation of new material to bring this book up to date. Her deepest thanks are due to Dr. Gordon R. Willey and Dr. John Honigmann, who took time during the 1960 International Congress of Americanists in Vienna to read Chapter XIV; both thanks and apologies are due to Dr. Joffre L. Coe, the first for his careful reading of the new material, the second because the revision was necessarily done in Europe, away from notes made during his interesting course on the American Indian at the University of North Carolina. To Louis Brennan, for his interest and generosity in checking successive drafts of the Preface and Chapter XIV; and to Hervey Chesley for stimulating suggestions and a critical reading of the manuscript, the author expresses grateful thanks. None of these is responsible for any misinterpretations that may have crept into the text. The author is indebted to Margaret Scoggin, Office of Young Adult Services, The New York Public Library, for assistance in bringing the Suggested Readings up to date.

INDEX